THE 100 BEST-SELLING
ALBUMS OF THE 60S

Gene Sculatti

igloo

This edition published in 2005 by Igloo Books Ltd
Henson Way
Telford Way Industrial Estate
Kettering NN16 8PX
info@igloo-books.com

ISBN: 1-904687-10-5

Editorial and design by:
Amber Books Ltd
Bradley's Close
74-77 White Lion Street
London N1 9PF
United Kingdom
www.amberbooks.co.uk

Editorial or design queries should be addressed to Amber Books Ltd

Printed in Singapore

ACKNOWLEDGEMENTS
Thanks to the following for help with researching and supplying the albums as well as for their invaluable industry knowledge:
Reckless Records (www.reckless.co.uk), Islington, London
Flashback (www.flashback.co.uk), Islington, London
Golden Grooves (www.goldengroovesrecords.com), Old Street, London
Haggle (www.hagglevinyl.com), Islington, London
The Music and Video Exchange, Notting Hill, London
Stage and Screen, Notting Hill, London
Beanos (www.beanos.co.uk)

'Featured CD titles available at HMV stores & hmv.co.uk'

©Apple Corps Ltd: The Beatles, pages 111, 129, 133, 169, 171, 185, 195, 197, 203, 205, 209, 211, 215.
©Abcko: The Rolling Stones, pages 71, 75, 109, 163.

Contents

Editor's foreword

The ranking of the 100 best-selling albums of the 1960s listed in the following pages is based upon the number of platinum and multi-platinum sales awards each album has achieved, as certified by the Recording Industry Association of America (RIAA). In an industry not always noted for the accuracy of its published sales figures, these awards provide one of the most effective and reliable ways to measure sales success. Each RIAA platinum award represents sales of at least 1,000,000 units, providing a consistent measure by which to rate the relative position of the decade's best-selling albums.

These figures also have the advantage – unlike similar lists based on chart position – of showing album sales from the date of first release right up to the present day, meaning the success of an album such as Led Zeppelin's eponymous debut, which only just made it into the US Top Ten on its release in 1969 but has sold consistently in every decade since, is properly reflected in its position.

Compilation or greatest hits albums are not included in this list, although live albums and original movie soundtracks, where all of the songs have been collected together or recorded specifically for the album, are included.

Ranking of equal sellers

Where two or more albums have the same sales total they are arranged by date of release, with the most recent album released ranked highest, since its sales are stronger relative to time spent on the market. Elvis Presley's 1960 album *GI Blues*, for example, has had almost a decade longer to obtain its platinum certification than The Doors' 1969 release *Soft Parade*, and is therefore ranked lower in the list.

Facts and figures

The appendices provide a breakdown of some of the most interesting facts and figures found throughout this book. You can find out which artists have the most albums in the list and who are the highest-ranking US and UK acts. You can see which albums have won the most Grammy awards or contain the most Number One singles, what were the best-selling soundtracks and live albums, and which record labels were the most successful of the decade.

Alongside tributes to old favourites there are enough surprises to keep the most dedicated music buff guessing. From 1960s icons such as The Rolling Stones and Jimi Hendrix to now more forgotten artists such as the Singing Nun or Sgt. Barry Sandler (whose collection of patriotic military ballads held The Rolling Stones off the top of the US charts for several weeks in 1966), the information contained in these lists should stimulate plenty of lively discussion. The albums are illustrated using a mixture of the US and UK sleeve designs – a selection that includes some of the most iconic images of the decade.

US and UK album sales

The lists in this book are based on US album sales. Consistent or reliable figures for UK sales in the 1960s are difficult to come by. The British Phonographic Industry (BPI) certification scheme only dates back to 1973 and multiple awards were not created until the mid-1980s. UK panel sales – figures based on sales to a limited number of retail outlets – date back only to 1969. The record companies themselves did not always release sales figures and where these figures do exist they are rarely up-to-date.

However, the sheer size of the US album market relative to that of other regions means the list does give an accurate picture of the decade's best-selling albums internationally. The large number of British bands in the list – eight of the top ten albums are by UK artists – shows the influence British music had throughout this period.

Composer Henry Mancini's soundtrack to the 1961 movie *Breakfast At Tiffany's* won five Grammy awards, more than any other album in the 100 best-selling albums of the 1960s.

The Best-Selling Albums of the 1960s

It's tempting to declare that the long-playing record came of age in the 1960s. In truth, the 1960s was when the format began acting much younger than its years. Throughout the 1950s, the 12-inch album had been adult record-buyers' more expansive, expensive format of choice. Younger consumers, especially rock 'n' roll-consuming teenagers, had to be content with the cheaper, more restrictive seven-inch single. Thirty minutes of content vs. three minutes of thrills.

All that had changed by the mid- and late-1960s. By the time album sales overtook singles in America in 1967, the LP's principal purchasers were teenagers, and the prevailing repertoire was pop and rock – not the soundtracks, Broadway show scores and easy-listening favourites of the 1950s. Indeed, rock-band recordings from the last third of the 1960s account for more than half of the decade's best-sellers. Scores and soundtrack albums represent barely a tenth.

Baby boomers and Beatlemania
This dramatic turn of events owed much to The Beatles, whose arrival supercharged both the business engine and the aural aesthetic of popular music. While such artists as The Beach Boys (with 1963's *Little Deuce Coupe*) and Peter, Paul & Mary (with their eponymous debut in 1962) occasionally scaled the upper reaches of the charts, The Beatles were so popular that all their albums sold as briskly as hit singles. In the first four months of 1964 alone, *Meet The Beatles!*, *Introducing The Beatles....*, *The Beatles' Second Album* and *The Beatles With Tony Sheridan* all charted in the US.

The musical revolution ignited by The Beatles and fuelled by vast numbers of cash-empowered 'baby boomers' led to an explosion of pop-rock albums in the mid-1960s. This renaissance is represented by works such as Dylan's *Blonde on Blonde* and *Highway 61 Revisited*, The Rolling Stones' *Aftermath* and *Out of Our Heads*, The Beach Boys' *Pet Sounds* and the Mamas And The Papas' *If You Can Believe Your Eyes and Ears*.

Repercussions and ambitions
The LP's 1967 ascent to dominant status, and the universal triumph of *Sgt. Pepper's Lonely Hearts Club Band* in particular (the album was Number One for 15 weeks), had profound consequences. The Beatles' album, clearly the most ambitious undertaking yet from the genre

that Frank Sinatra once called 'the most brutal, ugly, degenerate, vicious form of expression it has been my misfortune to hear', turned heads within the pop-music community and beyond. *Sgt. Pepper*'s critical and commercial triumph stung the Beach Boys' Brian Wilson (whose groundbreaking 1966 album *Pet Sounds* had been a huge inspiration to The Beatles) into announcing his intention to start work on an even grander experiment, *Smile*. In 1967 The Rolling Stones also tried to top The Beatles with their extravagant album *Their Satanic Majesties Request*. *Newsweek* magazine, meanwhile, lauded The Beatles as poets the equal of T.S. Eliot, Wordsworth and Tennyson.

No less significant for 1960s' music were the economic repercussions of the album's new-found prominence. Almost overnight, the recording industry went from a business whose chief revenues derived from sales of a unit priced at 79 to 99 cents (the seven-inch '45' single) to one priced at $3.98 (mono) and $4.98 (stereo). The increase in both price and sales volume funded all manner of expenditures at the record labels: the signing of more artists (for higher advances against royalties), bigger budgets for recording and marketing, and more staff to support these efforts – basically the model for the modern music business.

The complex arrangements and production techniques on The Beach Boys' 1966 album *Pet Sounds* showed the potential for what could be achieved with an ambitious and innovative approach to pop music.

Great expectations

Armed with new resources and inspiration, late-1960s musicians embarked on artistic ventures undreamed of only a few years before. Suddenly, there was a profusion of double albums (The Beatles' 'white' album, Cream's *Wheels of Fire*, Chicago's *Chicago Transit Authority*), rock operas

Cream's ambitious 1968 double-album set, *Wheels Of Fire*, showed their determination to break free from the confines of traditional rock and R&B.

(The Who's *Tommy*, the Broadway musical *Hair*) and even symphonic-rock collaborations (The Moody Blues' *Days of Future Passed*). Which is not to suggest that frivolous excess was the main legacy of late-1960s rock. These albums contained much highly innovative music and the freedom from prior restraints generated such musical milestones as Jimi Hendrix's *Are You Experienced?* and Van Morrison's *Moondance*.

The period is also memorable for expanding the musical parameters and array of subjects that pop music might address. As early as 1962–63, acutely political material was making its way up the charts thanks to Bob Dylan's *Freewheelin'* album and the Peter, Paul & Mary LP. By the later 1960s, such topics as sexual liberation (The Doors' 'Light My Fire'), social and personal alienation (Simon & Garfunkel's 'America') and race relations (Sly & The Family Stone's 'Don't Call Me Nigger, Whitey') were in the charts. Creedence Clearwater Revival's *Willie and the Poor Boys* contained the pointed draft protest (and Top-15 single) 'Fortunate Son.'

Genrefication

The massive commercial success of rock led to the development of whole new subgenres, each sparking its own hugely popular works. There was the West Coast acid-rock of bands such as

Big Brother & The Holding Co., Santana, Iron Butterfly and The Doors, and the roots-rock of Creedence Clearwater Revival. Led Zeppelin helped create the heavy-metal genre and bands such as Blood, Sweat & Tears and Chicago experimented with brass-assisted-rock. Meanwhile, Blind Faith pointed the way to the sort of 'supergroup' rock bands which would emerge in the 1970s.

Packaging and promotion

So great was the young public's appetite for the new music that a fresh radio format emerged to expose the wealth of releases that could not be accommodated by AM Top-40 stations with their restrictions on record length and subject matter. Although FM dates back to the 1940s, it is today radio's dominant band because 1960s 'underground' stations like New York's WOR, San Francisco's KMPX and the UK's Radio Caroline proved that underserved rock fans could comprise a profitable constituency for advertisers. Such stations, whose format later came to be called 'Album-Oriented Rock' (AOR), provided many listeners their introduction to artists like Jimi Hendrix, The Doors and Led Zeppelin.

Further fallout from the album-rock era was an increased attention to packaging. This can be seen in *Sgt. Pepper*'s photo collage, The Rolling

The UK sleeve for Hendrix's *Electric Ladyland* was considered so risqué that many shops sold the album in brown paper bags. Hendrix disliked the cover, complaining it detracted from the music, but his record company was happy with the controversy and publicity it brought.

Stones' 3D photo inset for *Their Satanic Majesties Request* and the silver-foil lamination used on the initial issues of Cream's *Wheels of Fire*. Another expression of this trend could be seen in the development of the promotional music video. While the 1970s are recognized rightly as the first proper music-video decade, the 1960s saw the creation of some of the first short promo videos, like the one for The Beatles' 'Penny Lane' or clips like 'Unknown Soldier' from The Doors' *Waiting For The Sun* LP. There were also experiments in more extensive cross-media promotions, such as The Beatles' feature film, *Magical Mystery Tour,* or The Monkees' television series, which ran for two seasons from 1966–68.

Buttoned-down sounds

It would be wrong, however, to peg the expansion of the 1960s music audience solely on the growing sophistication of rock. The numbers of commercially successful motion-picture scores and original-cast albums may have been dwarfed by the tally of rock LPs, but the former proved to have enduring appeal. President Kennedy's favourite, the soundtrack to the Broadway musical *Camelot*, remained on the Billboard chart for a staggering five years. Right behind it were *The Sound Of Music* soundtrack (four-and-a-half years) and the *Fiddler On The Roof* original-cast album and *Dr Zhivago* film score (both three years). In October 1961, the film soundtrack to *West Side Story* commenced a 54-week stay at Number One on the Billboard charts.

Also contributing significantly to the decade's bounty was the early- and mid-1960s comedy boom. Vaughn Meader's presidential sendup *The First Family* held its position at the top of the charts for 12 consecutive weeks. *The Button Down Mind of Bob Newhart* and Bill Cosby's *Bill Cosby Is a Very Funny Fellow Right!* also logged impressive performances.

Established artists

Through the mid-1960s, middle-of-the-road artists like Nat King Cole, Henry Mancini, Andy Williams, Ray Coniff and the Tijuana Brass sold well alongside their brasher companions, as did pop vocalists Sinatra and Streisand. Times grew leaner for most of these acts as the decade progressed, and by 1969 many of the easy-listening radio stations that had aired cuts from Streisand's *Funny Girl* or Williams' *Days of Wine and Roses* were gone, victims of the rock assault. But the 1950s' top album artist, Elvis Presley, still managed to notch up five of the decade's most popular albums – three soundtracks and the sacred-music collections *His Hand in Mine* and *How Great Thou Art*.

Crossover appeal

Later 1960s non-rock artists benefitted greatly from the expanded album-buying market, especially if they had some connection to the rock audience. Johnny Cash's *At Folsom Prison* and *At San Quentin* are a case in point. The singer's iconoclastic stance and irreverent material drew fans from the college crowd as much as it did older country-music fans, which helped boost sales of *Folsom* past the 3,000,000 mark. Ray Charles had achieved a similar crossover feat in 1962, corralling pop, R&B and country fans with *Modern Sounds in Country and Western Music*, a Number One for 14 weeks.

Glen Campbell – the last of the consistently successful male pop vocalists – enjoyed a run of four hit albums from 1967–69: *Gentle On My Mind*, *By The Time I Get To Phoenix*, *Wichita Lineman* and *Galveston*. Campbell had been a prominent studio musician on recordings by Phil Spector, The Beach Boys and The Monkees, and a certain hipness factor accrued to his repertoire, which featured songs by Jimmy Webb, Harry Nilsson and Donovan, among others. Campbell's occasional duet partner, Bobbie Gentry, also enjoyed a rock credibility (her Southern swamp-pop *Ode To Billie Joe* was a Number One album), which distinguished her from such 1960s one-shots as the Singing Nun and Sgt. Barry Sadler.

Glen Campbell's 1969 album *Galveston* showed that country melodies and traditional pop vocals could still appeal to the mainstream – although he also benefitted from a certain amount of rock credibility.

The big hitters

Looking at the numbers, it's clear that The Beatles dominated the decade. They placed 13 albums on the 1960s best-seller list, ending with their pensive, penultimate set, *Abbey Road*. Coming some way after The Beatles was the era's other most influential artist, Bob Dylan. His six 1960s hits travel an almost circular route from the rustic folk of *Freewheelin'* through the poetic hallucinations of *Highway 61 Revisited* back to the unvarnished country of *Nashville Skyline*.

The Monkees and Elvis Presley each earned five spots on the 100 best-selling albums list – demonstrating, perhaps, that there is always a demand for light entertainment. But even this interpretation is slightly misleading: Presley's tally includes the gospel albums *His Hand in Mine* and *How Great Thou Art* – strong personal statements that elicited some of the King's most committed performances.

Meanwhile albums like *The Monkees* or *The Birds, The Bees & The Monkees* simply deliver well-crafted pop that needs little other justification. After all, 'Pleasant Valley Sunday' (from The Monkees' 1968 album *Pisces, Aquarius, Capricorn & Jones*) doesn't get the edge over the band's other tracks for its trenchant social commentary, but for Mickey Dolenz's dazzling, joyous singing.

Artists charting with four album best-sellers range from pop vocalist Glen Campbell and literate-rock laureates Simon & Garfunkel to libertines The Doors and, of course, the band considered The Beatles' chief rivals throughout the decade, The Rolling Stones.

Late leaders

There are two further interesting aspects to the rankings of 1960s best-sellers. One is the high placement of the albums *Led Zeppelin* and *Led Zeppelin II* – coming in at Number Five and Number Two, respectively. The achievement is underscored by the fact that both were issued in the last year of the decade and had to muscle aside the entries of many artists who'd been around much longer. The proof is in the numbers. Between them, the two Led Zeppelin albums have sold in excess of 22,000,000 copies.

Also remarkable is the fact that the list contains only one Motown album, the Supremes and Temptations' *TCB*. Throughout the decade the 1960's pre-eminent pop-soul label continued to focus on hit singles, rather than albums. It would not be until the early 1970s that Motown would post a serious number of LP best-sellers on the charts – Stevie Wonder's *Talking Book*, Fulfillingness' *First Finale* and Marvin Gaye's *What's Goin' On* and *Let's Get It On*.

The long-play legacy

In all discussions of the 1960s, one thing is certain: after it, nothing would ever be the same again. Popular music changed radically during the decade; while tuneful, radio-friendly singles never disappeared, they took on new travelling companions – and baggage.

In 1959, the Recording Industry Association of America (RIAA) reported total phonograph-record sales of $603 million. By 1969, these sales had reached almost $1.6 billion. The rise in the popularity of the long-playing album – and the prosperous baby-boomer generation that came of age along with this rise – were the principal source of this increase. The new album format provided pop musicians with a whole new palette in which to work and raised questions about just how much they might attempt in the pop medium. Grand works and follies, misfires and masterpieces have been the answer, and all have contributed to a fascinating cultural experience that continues four decades later.

The sales figures for the decade suggest that in the 1960s, the public's musical expectations were being met, regularly and richly. And that so many of the albums of the 1960s continue to be bought today – in many cases by members of generations unborn at the time of the records' initial release – says even more than the statistics.

TCB, The Supremes and The Temptations' soundtrack to their 1968 television-special, is the only Motown album in the 100 best-selling albums. One wonders what could have been achieved had the label chosen to promote more of their artists across the range of media available in the 1960s.

The Button-Down Mind Of Bob Newhart

| • **Album sales:** 500,000 | • **Release date:** 1960 |

Among other distinctions, Bob Newhart can claim the honour of having made the first comedy album to top the Billboard charts. *The Button-Down Mind,* recorded live at the Tidelands Club, Houston, Texas, also won a Grammy for 1960s Best Album.

The achievement of *The Button-Down Mind* becomes even greater when the richness of the competition is considered. Newhart, the quiet Chicago accountant-turned-standup comic, was working for laughs in the same late-1950s/early-1960s arena as Shelley Berman, Lenny Bruce, Mort Sahl and Jonathan Winters. Newhart's comedy was gentler and more cerebral than that of his peers, often putting historical figures into contemporary contexts for the purpose of critiquing modern mass culture. Typical of these are the *Button-Down Mind* routines speculating on how contemporary marketers might promote such challenging 'products' as Abraham Lincoln and the Wright brothers.

The album saved the fledgling Warner Bros. Records label, which soon grew into a major international corporation. Successive albums like *The Button-Down Mind Strikes Back!* (another Number One) and *Behind the Button-Down Mind* expanded Newhart's touring schedule and television appearances and eventually led to two successful sitcoms, 'The Bob Newhart Show' (1972 to 1978) and 'Newhart' (1982 to 1990).

Number One singles: None	**Recorded in:** Houston, USA
Grammy awards: Album of the year; Best new artist	**Personnel:** Bob Newhart
Label: US & UK: Warner	**Producers:** N/A

1 Abe Lincoln Vs Madison Avenue (7:31)
2 Cruise Of The USS *Codfish* (5:01)
3 Merchandizing The Wright Brothers (3:12)
4 Khrushchev Landing Rehearsal (4:47)
5 Driving Instructor (8:03)
6 Nobody Will Ever Play Baseball (3:21)

Total album length: 32 minutes

THE BUTTON-DOWN MIND OF BOB NEWHART

MONO | WM 4010

WARNER BROS.
1379 · HIGH FIDELITY

THE MOST CELEBRATED NEW COMEDIAN SINCE ATTILA
(THE HUN)

THE BUTTON-DOWN MIND OF
BOB NEWHART

Breakfast At Tiffany's

| • **Album sales:** 500,000 | • **Release date:** 1961 |

Although it's but one of many soundtracks by the prolific composer, Mancini's *Breakfast At Tiffany's* album occupies a special place. It was his first Number One LP since 1959's *Peter Gunn* soundtrack and is introduced by what is probably Mancini's most memorable composition.

'Moon River' has endured countless interpretations – by pop vocalists, jazz combos, chorales and R&B artists. In 1961, Mancini and Chicago's 'Ice Man', Jerry Butler, each took single versions of the song into the Top 20. The haunting tune rightly won a Grammy for Best soundtrack for film or television. In comparison, the rest of *Breakfast* could be said to pale

against 'Moon River'. Actually, like most Mancini scores, it's – to borrow a phrase from one of his Peter Gunn tracks – 'A Profound Gass'.

If he wasn't already America's foremost film-music composer, Mancini certainly grew into the role following *Breakfast at Tiffany's*, going on to record such milestone scores as *Charade*, *Days of Wine and Roses* and the *Pink Panther* series.

Number One singles: None

Grammy Awards: Record of the year – Moon River; Song of the year –Moon River; Best performance by an orchestra; Best arrangement – Moon River; Best soundtrack or score from motion picture or television.

Label: US & UK: RCA

Recorded in: Hollywood, USA

Personnel: Henry Mancini (d. 1994)

Producers: Akira Taguchi Dick Pierce

1 Moon River (2:46)
2 Something For The Cat (3:11)
3 Sally's Tomato (3:09)
4 Mr Yunioshi (2:32)
5 Big Blow Out (2:30)
6 Hub Caps And Tail Lights (2:33)
7 Breakfast At Tiffany's (2:49)
8 Latin Golightly (3:00)
9 Holly (3:21)
10 Loose Caboose (3:11)
11 Big Heist (3:10)
12 Moon River (Cha Cha) (2:35)
13 Arabesque (2:16)
14 We've Loved Before / Yasmine's Theme (Instrumental) (2:55)

15 Ascot (1:55)
16 Dream Street (3:53)
17 Facade (3:19)
18 Something For Sophia (2:36)
19 We've Loved Before / Yasmine's Theme (Vocal) (2:48)
20 Shower Of Paradise / The Zoo Chase (2:36)
21 Pt 1: Arabesque Theme (2:19)
22 Pt 2: Aquarium Scene (2:28)
23 Pt 3: Arabesque Theme (Reprise) (1:02)
24 Bagdad On The Thames (3:03)

Total album length: 66 minutes

"Breakfast at Tiffany's" A PARAMOUNT PICTURE

MUSIC FROM THE MOTION PICTURE SCORE COMPOSED AND CONDUCTED BY

HENRY MANCINI

Modern Sounds In Country & Western Music

| • **Album sales:** 500,000 | • **Release date:** June 1962 |

'**W**asn't trying to change the world. Just wanted to sing songs I loved.' That's how Ray Charles explained the intent behind *Modern Sounds In Country and Western Music*, in his notes to 1997's *Genius & Soul* anthology.

To some observers, the album signified a bold left turn for a respected figure who'd built his career on soulful rock 'n' roll, slick urban R&B and a well-received jazz LP with Count Basie's band. The success of *Modern Sounds* validated Charles' instincts and gave him his first chart-topping album. It is also credited with helping to popularize country-music around the world.

Charles' supple voice and the chorale and strings accompaniment made pop smashes of Don Gibson's 'I Can't Stop Loving You', Eddy Arnold's 'You Don't Know Me' and Ted Daffan's 'Born to Lose', three of the Hot 100s most affecting ballads. The album opener, Felice and Boudleaux Bryant's first Everly Bros. hit, 'Bye Bye Love', swings madly, thanks to a kinetic performance by Charles' band.

So popular was the album that Charles recorded *Modern Sounds (Volume Two)* later the same year. It also clicked with pop audiences, generating Top 10 singles in 'You Are My Sunshine' and 'Your Cheating Heart'.

Number One singles:
US & UK: I Can't Stop Loving You

Grammy awards:
Best R&B recording

Label: US: ABC Paramount; UK: HMV

Recorded in: N/A

Personnel:
Ray Charles
Hank Crawford

Producer: N/A

1 Bye Bye Love (2:12)
2 You Don't Know Me (3:16)
3 Half As Much (3:28)
4 I Love You So Much It Hurts (3:35)
5 Just A Little Lovin' (3:29)
6 Born To Lose (3:18)
7 Worried Mind (2:57)
8 It Makes No Difference Now (3:36)
9 You Win Again (3:31)
10 Careless Love (4:01)
11 I Can't Stop Loving You (4:14)
12 Hey, Good Lookin' (2:14)

Total album length: 40 minutes

Ray Charles

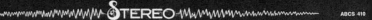

STEREO

ABCS 410

RAY CHARLES

MODERN SOUNDS
IN COUNTRY AND
WESTERN MUSIC

GOLD RECORD AWARD

ABC-PARAMOUNT
Full Color Fidelity

The First Family

| **Album sales:** 500,000 | **Release date:** November 1962 |

It's perhaps no surprise that there never were any President 'Ike' Eisenhower impersonators. But, once the charismatic John F. Kennedy and his clan swept into the White House, the young president with the Boston accent became a magnet for mimicry.

The most successful comedic Kennedy clone was Vaughn Meader, an impressionist recruited by comedy writers Bob Booker and Earle Doud to star in an album satirizing the new president. Meader, a Bostonian who'd actually attended the same high school as his subject, does a first-rate JFK, while supporting cast members handle the family and various dignitaries of the day. Over the album's two 'Acts', Meader, as Kennedy, holds forth at a press conference, orders deli food for a lunch with world leaders and discusses his daughter Caroline's allowance.

The album held onto Billboard's Number One slot for 12 consecutive weeks in 1962, winning that year's Grammy for Best Album. A second *First Family* LP was issued in mid-1963, but Kennedy's assassination that November put an end to the role that made Meader a celebrity. He later managed a restaurant in the Boston area.

Number One singles:
None

Grammy awards: Album of the year; Best comedy performance

Label: US: Cadence; UK: London

Recorded in: New York, USA

Personnel:
Vaughn Meader
Naomi Brussart
George Foster
Jim Lehner
Norma MacMillan

Producers:
Bob Booker
Earle Doud

1 The Experiment (0:44)
2 After Dinner Conversations (4:58)
3 The Malayan Ambassador (0:59)
4 Relatively Speaking (0:38)
5 Astronauts (0:58)
6 Motorcade (0:48)
7 The Party (0:45)
8 The Tour (6:35)
9 But Vote!! (0:22)
10 Economy Lunch (5:16)
11 The Decision (1:19)
12 White House Visitor (0:57)
13 Press Conference (2:36)
14 The Dress (1:07)
15 Saturday Night, Sunday Morning (4:16)
16 Auld Lang Syne (1:19)
17 Bedtime Story (1:42)

Total album length: 35 minutes

Vaughn Meader

96 Days Of Wine And Roses

| • **Album sales:** 500,000 | • **Release date:** January 1963 |

The harrowing world of alcohol addiction provided the source for one of the 1960s' most popular easy-listening records. Williams' version of Henry Mancini's theme from the 1962 film *Days of Wine and Roses* (starring Jack Lemmon as a desperate drunk) was a big hit as a single, spawning this album.

Williams' only chart-topper, *Days Of Wine And Roses* shows why he was, after Perry Como and before Glen Campbell, America's favorite male vocalist. The title song is the album's high point, with the remaining tracks, as was customary, offering Williams' respectful treatments of standards of the day. Tony Bennett's 'I Left My Heart In San Francisco', Sammy Davis. Jr.'s 'What Kind Of Fool Am I' and Kitty Kallen's 'My Coloring Book' had barely slipped off the charts when *Days* was recorded.

The album's most adventurous selection is 'Can't Get Used To Losing You'. The space-filled mid-tempo ballad, written by pop-rock tunesmiths Doc Pomus and Mort Schuman ('This Magic Moment', 'Little Sister', 'Teenager in Love'), was a Number Two single that initiated a string of four moderately rocking Top 40 hits for Williams. The album remained on Billboard's LP chart for 107 weeks.

1 Falling In Love With Love (2:12)
2 I Left My Heart In San Francisco (3:05)
3 You Are My Sunshine (2:29)
4 What Kind Of Fool Am I? (3:22)
5 When You're Smiling (1:44)
6 Days Of Wine And Roses (2:47)
7 It's A Most Unusual Day (2:03)
8 My Coloring Book (3:33)
9 Can't Get Used To Losing You (2:24)
10 I Really Don't Want To Know (2:54)
11 Exactly Like You (1:59)
12 May Each Day (2:53)
13 Very Thought Of You (2:42)
14 If I Love Again (2:32)

Total album length: 37 minutes

Number One singles: None	**Recorded in:** N/A
Grammy Awards: None	**Personnel:** Andy Williams
Label: US & UK: Columbia	**Producer:** Robert Mersey

Andy Williams

STEREO
CS 8815

MONAURAL—CL 2015
COLUMBIA

ANDY WILLIAMS

Days of Wine and Roses
And Other TV Requests

CAN'T GET USED TO
LOSING YOU

DAYS OF
WINE AND ROSES

FALLING IN LOVE
WITH LOVE

MY COLORING BOOK

WHAT KIND OF FOOL
AM I?

I LEFT MY HEART
IN SAN FRANCISCO

WHEN YOU'RE SMILING

I REALLY DON'T
WANT TO KNOW

YOU ARE MY SUNSHINE

IT'S A MOST UNUSUAL
DAY

EXACTLY LIKE YOU

MAY EACH DAY

Produced by Robert Mersey

95 The Singing Nun

| • **Album sales:** 500,000 | • **Release date:** November 1963 |

The Singing Nun occupied a place in religio-pop roughly midway between the Mormon Tabernacle Choir (*The Lord's Prayer*, 1959) and the Benedictine Monks of Santo Domingo de Silos (*Chant*, 1994). In 1963, Belgian Sister Luc-Gabrielle (née Jeanine Deckers), accompanying herself on guitar, recorded some of her original songs, intending to make them available as gifts to friends. A tape of her music found its way to Phillips Records, the Netherlands' largest label, which, impressed, signed Luc-Gabrielle and issued her song 'Dominique' as a single under the stage name Soeur Sourire, or 'Sister Smile'.

The record quickly became an international best-seller, hitting the top of the Hot 100 in the same year as a number of folk-flavoured discs by Peter, Paul & Mary, The Rooftop Singers and The New Christy Minstrels. 'Dominique' was succeeded by *The Singing Nun* album, which contained the hit and 11 more of the nun's originals, sung in French but translated into English inside the record's gatefold. The album also hit the US Number One, where it resided for 10 straight weeks.

By 1966, the Singing Nun had left the music field and returned in order to fund a school she had established for autistic children. In 1985, beset with personal problems and difficulties with her school, she committed suicide.

1 Dominique (2:53)
2 Soeur Adele (4:25)
3 Fleur De Cactus (1:47)
4 Complainte De Marie-Jacques (2:24)
5 Je Voudrais (1:52)
6 Tous Les Chemins (2:33)
7 Plume De Radis (1:57)
8 Mets Ton Joli Jupon (1:26)
9 Resurrection (3:45)
10 Alleluia (2:50)
11 J'ai Trouve Le Seigneur (2:54)
12 Entre Les Etioles (3:13)

Total album length: 33 minutes

Number One singles:
US: Dominique

Grammy Awards: Best gospel or other religious recording (musical)

Label: US & UK: Philips

Recorded in: N/A

Personnel:
Sister Luc-Gabrielle (d. 1985)

Producer:
Gordon Anderson

Soeur Sourire

SOEUR SOURIRE **THE SINGING NUN**

CONNOISSEUR COLLECTION PHILIPS

PHILIPS

Sleeve artwork by Soeur Sourire

94 Mary Poppins

| • **Album sales:** 500, 000 | • **Release date:** August 1964 |

The soundtrack to the top-grossing motion picture of 1964 also delivered a stellar performance. *Mary Poppins* was Billboard's top-ranked album for 14 weeks, staying on the chart for more than two years. The film was nominated for 13 Academy Awards, winning five, including Best Actress for star Julie Andrews.

The story of nanny Mary (Andrews) and her magical adventures with the children of the Banks family was the occasion for one of the most captivating scores by the acclaimed songwriting team of Richard and Robert Sherman. The best known selection is the nonsensical secret-word song, 'Supercalifragilisticexpialidocious'. Sung by

Andrews with co-star Dick Van Dyke and released as a single, it made the Hot 100 chart in 1965. 'A Spoonful of Sugar (Helps The Medicine Go Down)', the spirited ode to finding fun in one's work, is another album highlight, as is Van Dyke's chimney-sweep anthem, 'Chim Chim Cher-ee', delivered in a not-entirely-convincing Cockney accent. The irresistibly melodic song was a Top 20 easy-listening hit for the New Christy Minstrels in 1965.

Number One singles: None

Grammy awards: None

Label: US: EMI; UK: HMV

Recorded in: California, USA

Producer: Ronnie Kidd

Personnel:
Julie Andrews
David Tomlinson
Dick Van Dyke
Ed Wynn
Elsa Lanchester
Glynis Johns
Herminone Baddeley
Karen Dotrice
Matthew Garber
Irwin Kostal

1　Overture (3:01)
2　Sister Suffragette (2:03)
3　Life I Lead (1:45)
4　Perfect Nanny (2:02)
5　Spoonful Of Sugar (1:39)
6　Pavement Artist (4:09)
7　Jolly Holiday (2:00)
8　Supercalifragilistic-expialidocious (5:24)
9　Stay Awake (1:45)
10　I Love To Laugh (2:44)
11　British Bank (2:08)
12　Feed The Birds (3:51)

13　Fidelity Fiduciary Bank (3:33)
14　Chim Chim Cher-ee (2:46)
15　Step In Time (8:43)
16　Medley: Man Has Dreams (The Life I Lead)/A Spoonful of Sugar (4:29)
17　Let's Go Fly A Kite (1:54)
18　Sherman Brothers Reminisce: Chim Chim Cher-ee/Let's Go Fly A Kite (16:07)

Total album length: 70 minutes

Original Soundtrack

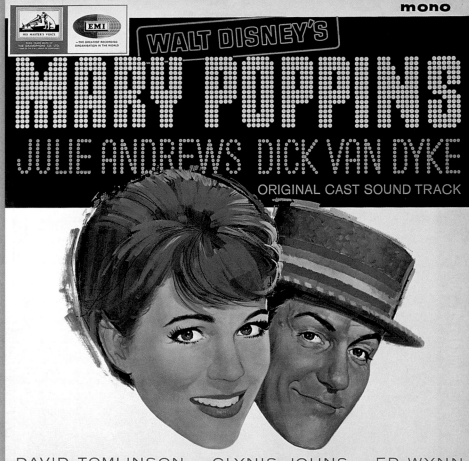

93 Goldfinger

| • **Album sales:** 500,000 | • **Release date:** October 1964 |

John Barry's score for one of the most popular James Bond films was a cornerstone of what a later age would designate 'lounge music', or, more specifically, 'spy jazz'. The *Goldfinger* soundtrack was America's best-selling album for three weeks at the end of 1964 and the first Bond score to hit Number One.

The soundtrack album is best remembered for its opening track, Shirley Bassey's torchy vocal version of the main theme, which became a Top 10 single. Most of the rest of the (instrumental) selections are adaptations of the principal theme – as a jazz waltz, galloping martial charge, hide-and-seek chase music – often punctuated by jarring brass accents and rumbling kettle drums.

Although his scoring credentials go back to the 1960 UK feature 'Beat Girl' and through the 1990s with such films as 'Born Free' (which won Grammy awards for 1966's Best Score and Best Song) and 'Dances With Wolves' (the 1991 Grammy for Best Composition for Motion Picture or Television), Barry's legacy remains inextricably bound to his Bond work. In addition to *Goldfinger*, he composed the scores for *Dr. No* (1962), *From Russia With Love* (1963), *You Only Live Twice* (1967), *Diamonds Are Forever* (1972) and *Moonraker* (1979).

Number One singles:
None

Grammy awards: None

Label: US & UK: EMI

Recorded in: N/A

Personnel:
John Barry
Shirley Bassey

Producer:
Harry Saltzman

1 Goldfinger (Sung By Shirley Bassey) Into Miami (2:47)
2 Alpin Drive – Auric's Factory (5:24)
3 Oddjob's Pressing Engagement (3:05)
4 Bond Back In Action Again (2:29)
5 Teasing The Korean (2:12)
6 Gassing The Gangsters (1:03)
7 Goldfinger (Instrumental Version) (2:08)
8 Dawn Raid On Fort Knox (5:43)
9 The Arrival Of The Bomb And Count Down (3:25)
10 The Death Of Goldfinger (2:34)

Total album length: 31 minutes

Original Soundtrack

ORIGINAL MOTION PICTURE SOUND TRACK

007 IAN FLEMING'S GOLDFINGER

MUSIC COMPOSED, ARRANGED AND CONDUCTED BY
john barry

TITLE SONG SUNG BY
shirley bassey

LYRICS BY
LESLIE BRICUSSE & ANTHONY NEWLEY

UNITED ARTISTS RECORDS

STEREO

HIGH FIDELITY GOLDFINGER · UNITED ARTISTS UAL 4117
STEREO UAS 5117

Roustabout

| • **Album sales:** 500,000 | • **Release date:** November 1964 |

A cute class-consciousness is probably the last thing you'd expect to find on an Elvis Presley soundtrack, but there it is, on his eighth Number One album. In *Roustabout*, Presley is Charlie Rogers, a young singer who joins a travelling circus and revives its sagging fortunes. When Charlie meets his nemesis in Sam the college student, it's the occasion to turn up the heat on the elite. In 'Hard Knocks' Presley opines that 'Some kids born with a silver spoon/ I guess I was born a little too soon', and in the ragtime rocker 'Poison Ivy League' he rails against those

'sons of the rich' whose well-placed parents get them into good colleges and cushy jobs.

Less socially relevant but suitably entertaining are the title track and 'Wheels On My Heels', typical of the infectious pop-rockers that populate most Presley soundtracks of the period. A cover of the Coasters' 'Little Egypt' finds Presley in even better form. 'Brand New Day on the Horizon' is a cha-cha-fied appropriation of the melody from 'Battle Hymn of the Republic'.

The movie itself, Presley's eleventh in seven years, wasn't as successful as *Viva Las Vegas*, also released in 1964. In the rankings of the year's top-grossing films, *Roustabout* barely edged into the Top 30.

Number One singles:
None

Grammy awards: None

Label: US & UK: RCA

Recorded in: California, USA

Personnel:
Elvis Presley (d. 1977)
Scotty Moore
Tiny Timbrell
Billy Strange

Bob Moore
Ray Siegal
DJ Fontana
Hal Blaine
Buddy Harman
Berne Mattinson
Floyd Cramer
Dudley Brookes
Boots Randolf
The Jordinaires
Mello Man

Producers: N/A

1   **Roustabout (1:57)**
2   **Little Egypt (2:17)**
3   **Poison Ivy League (2:01)**
4   **Hard Knocks (1:42)**
5   **It's A Wonderful World (1:48)**
6   **Big Love Heartache (1:58)**
7   **There's A Brand New Day On The Horizon (2:00)**
8   **Wheels On My Heels (1:19)**
9   **Carny Town (1:09)**
10 **One Track Heart (2:15)**
11 **It's Carnival Time (1:30)**

Total album length: 20 minutes

91 The Sound Of Music

| • Album sales: 500,000 | • Release date: March 1965 |

The Sound Of Music was one of the 1960s biggest film blockbusters, and the soundtrack to the saga of the Austrian Trapp Family Singers was one of the decade's most popular scores. A Number One album, the *The Sound Of Music* occupied slots on the Billboard album chart for a staggering four and a half years.

The score, by the legendary team of Richard Rodgers and Oscar Hammerstein II, covers considerable ground in its breadth of material. The songs range in style from the inspirational 'Climb Ev'ry Mountain' to the children's classic 'Do-Re-Mi' to the sophisticated pop jazz of 'My Favourite Things', here a *tour de force* for Julie Andrews (as Maria Von Trapp). 'My Favourite Things' became an instant classic. Not only did jazz giant John Coltrane turn it into his signature piece, but the song found its way onto albums by artists as diverse as Dave Brubeck, The Carpenters and Barbra Streisand.

'Climb Ev'ry Mountain,' performed on the soundtrack by Peggy Wood (as the Mother Abbess), has been recorded by Placido Domingo, The Four Tops and Billy Eckstine.

Number One singles:	Charmain Carr
None	Debbis Turner
	Duane Chase
Grammy Awards: None	Heather Menzies
	Kim Karath
Label: US & UK: RCA	Nicholas Hammond
	Peggy Wood
Recorded in: N/A	Irwin Kostal

Personnel:	Producers:
Julie Andrews	Neely Plumb
Christopher Plummer	Saul Chaplin
Angela Cartwright	

1 Prelude / The Sound Of Music (2:46)
2 Overture & Preludium (Dixit Dominus) (3:15)
3 Morning Hymn / Alleludia (2:04)
4 Maria (3:19)
5 I Have Confidence (3:28)
6 Sixteen Going On Seventeen (3:20)
7 My Favourite Things (2:20)
8 Do-Re-Mi (5:35)
9 The Sound Of Music (2:13)
10 Lonely Goatherd (3:12)
11 So Long, Farewell (2:56)
12 Climb Ev'ry Mountain (2:18)
13 Something Good (3:19)
14 Processional / Maria (2:29)
15 Edleweiss (1:52)
16 Climb Ev'ry Mountain (Reprise) (1:20)

Total album length: 49 minutes

Original Soundtrack

Dr. Zhivago

| • **Album sales:** 500,000 | • **Release date:** December 1965 |

Maurice Jarre's score for *Dr. Zhivago*, his second film assignment for director David Lean, won an Oscar and peaked at Number One during an astonishing three-year run on the US albums chart. Set against the backdrop of the Russian Revolution, the adaptation of Pasternak's story of the romance between Zhivago (Omar Sharif) and his mistress (Julie Christie) required the French composer-conductor to work in a wide array of musical styles.

Jarre had just six weeks to complete the demanding project but succeeded masterfully, using a resourceful – and sizable – cast of supporting players: 110 symphonic musicians, 24 balalaika players and a chorale. The score's best remembered track is the lilting 'Lara's Theme'.

Number One singles:
None

Grammy awards:
Best original score written for a motion picture or television show

Label: US & UK: MGM Records

Recorded in: N/A

Personnel:
Maurice Jarre
Leo Arnaud
Monique Rollin

Producer:
Bradley Flanagan
Jessey Kaye

1 Overture (4:22)
2 Main Title (2:38)
3 Kontakion/Funeral Song (3:15)
4 Lara Is Charming (1:16)
5 Internationale (1:12)
6 Lara and Komarovsky Dancing Up A Storm (0:40)
7 Komarovsky And Lara In The Hotel (3:51)
8 Interior Student Cafe (1:34)
9 Sventitsky's Waltz/After the Shooting (2:17)
10 Military Parade (2:11)
11 They Began To Go Home (2:06)
12 After Deserters Killed The Colonel (1:05)
13 At The Hospital (1:00)
14 Lara Says Goodbye To Yuri (1:27)
15 Tonya Greets Yuri (0:46)
16 Stove's Out (1:30)
17 Yevgraf Snaps His Fingers (3:09)
18 Evening Bells/Moscow Station (1:03)
19 Flags Flying Over The Train (1:04)
20 Yuri Gazing Through A Tiny Open Hatch (0:36)
21 Door Banged Open (1:50)
22 Intermission (0:45)
23 Yuri Follows The Sound Of The Waterfall (0:42)
24 Tonya And Yuri Arrive At Varykino (2:53)
25 They Didn't Lock The Cottage (1:34)
26 Varykino Cottage (0:56)
27 Yuri And The Daffodils (1:16)
28 On A Yuriatin Street (1:33)
29 In Lara's Bedroom (0:31)
30 Yuri Rides To Yuriatin (0:23)
31 Yuri Is Taken Prisoner By The Red Partisans (0:48)
32 For As Long As We Need You (0:41)
33 Yuri Is Escaping (2:19)
34 Yuri Approaches Lara's Apartment (0:49)
35 Yuri Looks In The Mirror (0:31)
36 Lara And Yuri Arriving At Varykino (1:40)
37 Yuri Is Trying To Write (1:20)
38 Yuri Frightens The Wolves Away (0:48)
39 Lara Reads Her Poem (0:38)
40 Yuri Frightens The Wolves Away (Pt 2) (1:54)
41 Yuri Works On (0:52)
42 Then It's A Gift (1:46)
43 Lara's Theme (Jazz Version) (1:57)
44 Lara's theme (Rock 'N' Roll Version) (2:39)
45 Lara's Theme (Swing Version) (1:15)

Total album length: 69 minutes

M-G-M
LONG PLAYING
33⅓ R.P.M. RECORD

mono

THE ORIGINAL SOUND TRACK ALBUM

METRO-GOLDWYN-MAYER PRESENTS A CARLO PONTI PRODUCTION
DAVID LEAN'S FILM OF BORIS PASTERNAK'S

DOCTOR ZHIVAGO

Music composed and conducted by Maurice Jarre

Ballads Of The Green Berets

| **Album sales:** 500,000 | **Release date:** March 1966 |

Vietnam vet Sadler held The Rolling Stones off the top of the charts for several weeks. Their *Aftermath* stuck at Number Two while Sadler's patriotic *Ballads Of The Green Berets* remained at Number One for five weeks in the spring of 1966. The album duplicated the chart success of its namesake single, which praised America's elite Marine forces. A follow-up single, 'The 'A' Team', was a Top 30 hit.

Sadler's style varies little over the course of the album. Mid-tempo country songs dominate, with 'Lullaby' and the folk-flavoured 'Bamiba' providing the sole breaks. Tracks like 'Saigon' and 'Trooper's Lament' somewhat recall the early-1960s historical story-songs of Johnny Horton and Jimmy Dean. 'I'm the Lucky One' and 'The Soldier Has Come Home' address the return of the war's survivors and their not so lucky counterparts.

Sadler embarked on an unfruitful career as a straight-ahead country music singer in the 1970s, then became a successful author of a series of military adventure novels. He died in 1989. 'Ballad Of The Green Berets' was featured in the 1968 John Wayne film, *The Green Berets*.

Number One singles:
US: Ballad Of The Green Berets

Grammy Awards: None

Label: US & UK: RCA Victor

Recorded in: N/A

Personnel:
SSgt Barry Sadler (d. 1989)
Sid Bass

Producers:
Andy Wiswell

1   The Ballad Of The Green Berets (2:26)
2   Letter From Vietnam (2:29)
3   I'm A Lucky One (2:52)
4   Garet Trooper (2:35)
5   The Soldier Come Home (2:50)
6   Salute To The Nurses (2:20)
7   I'm Watching Raindrops Fall (2:08)
8   Badge Of Courage (2:30)
9   Trooper's Lament (2:30)
10 Bamiba (2:34)
11 Saigon (2:27)
12 Lullaby (3:10)

Total album length: 31 minutes

SSgt Barry Sadler

Ballads of the Green Berets

SSgt Barry Sadler

U.S. Army Special Forces

The Ballad of the Green Berets
Letter from Vietnam
I'm a Lucky One
Garet Trooper
The Soldier Has Come Home
Salute to the Nurses
I'm Watching the Raindrops Fall
Badge of Courage
Trooper's Lament
Bamiba
Saigon
Lullaby

Arranged and Conducted by
Sid Bass

If You Can Believe Your Eyes And Ears

| • **Album sales:** 500,000 | • **Release date:** June 1966 |

The Mama's & The Papa's made one of the noisiest arrivals of 1966, when their easy-listening 'California Dreamin' became a million-selling single. It's one of two million-sellers on the group's debut album. 'Monday Monday', likewise penned by leader John Phillips, rose to Number One on the US charts (reaching Number Three in the UK).

John Phillips, Cass Elliott, Denny Doherty and Michelle Phillips formed the group after several previous folk groups failed. Their roots in commercial folk music (Phillips was in the moderately successful Journeymen) show throughout *If You Can Believe Your Eyes And Ears*, but it's Phillips' deft ear for melody and way with the pop hook that give the music its appeal. The interweaving vocals that characterize the two singles and 'Go Where You Wanna Go' are exhilarating, and they provided the template for the group's subsequent hit streak, which lasted only another year.

The Mama's & The Papa's released only two more new albums (greatest-hits collections began appearing as early as 1967), then disbanded in 1968. Solo careers followed, though only Elliot achieved much success. Intermittent reunions, comprised of shifting line-ups, commenced in 1971.

Number one singles:
US: Monday, Monday

Grammy Awards: None

Label: US: Dunhill;
UK: RCA

Recorded in: N/A

Personnel:
John Phillips (d. 2001)
Cass Elliot (d. 1974)
Michelle Gilliam
Denny Doherty

Producer:
Lou Adler

1 Do You Wanna Dance (2:58)
2 Go Where You Wanna Go (2:32)
3 California Dreamin' (2:32)
4 Spanish Harlem (3:22)
5 Somebody Groovy (3:14)
6 Hey Girl (2:21)
7 You Baby (2:15)
8 In Crowd (3:10)
9 Monday Monday (3:03)
10 Straight Shooter (2:59)
11 Got A Feelin' (2:44)
12 I Call Your Name (2:32)

Total album length: 34 minutes

The Mama's And The Papa's

87 Sounds Like

| **Album sales:** 500,000 | **Release date:** June 1967 |

The success of *Sounds Like* gives some indication of just how popular Alpert's instrumental ensemble was with American audiences in the 1960s. The group's eighth LP, *Sounds Like,* gave the Tijuana Brass their fourth Number One album.

Sounds Like doesn't stray significantly from most Tijuana Brass collections, offering a pleasing selection of original songs and covers of familiar material. In the latter category are Burt Bacharach's theme from the then new James Bond feature, 'Casino Royale', and a clever arrangement of the gospel chestnut 'Wade in the Water'. Both cuts became Top 40 hits. The most

unusual cover is a fast treatment of Gene Pitney's 1961 hit 'Town Without Pity' that rather resembles the band's earlier breakneck take on 'Zorba the Greek'. 'Lady Godiva' had been a Top 10 single for Peter & Gordon in 1966, and 'In a Little Spanish Town' had been recorded by many pre-rock pop vocalists, including Bing Crosby.

Among the band originals, guitarist John Pisano contributes the light, breezy 'Charmer', and marimba player Julius Wechter serves up the wistful ballad 'Shades of Blue'. Longtime Brass writers Sol Lake and Erv Coleman deliver 'Bo Bo' and 'Miss Frenchy Brown', respectively.

Number One singles:
None

Grammy awards: None

Label: US & UK: A&M Records

Recorded in: N/A

Personnel:
Herb Alpert
Tonni Kalash
Bob Edmondson
Lou Pagani
John Pisano
Nick Ceroli
Julius Wechter (d. 1999)

Producers:
Herb Alpert
Jerry Moss

1 **Gotta Lotta Livin' To Do** (2:47)
2 **Lady Godiva** (2:06)
3 **Bo-Bo** (3:04)
4 **Shades Of Blue** (2:44)
5 **In A Little Spanish Town** (1:54)
6 **Wade In The Water** (3:03)
7 **Town Without Pity** (2:14)
8 **The Charmer** (2:13)
9 **Treasure Of San Miguel** (2:14)
10 **Miss Frenchy Brown** (2:27)
11 **Casino Royale** (2:35)

Total album length: 27 minutes

...SOUNDS LIKE...
HERB ALPERT
The TIJUANA BRASS

CASINO ROYALE
WADE IN THE WATER
GOTTA LOTTA LIVIN' TO DO
TOWN WITHOUT PITY
IN A LITTLE SPANISH TOWN
LADY GODIVA

A&M
RECORDS

86 Ode To Billie Joe

| • **Album sales:** 500,000 | • **Release date:** June 1967 |

Gentry's place in pop was secured by the monstrous hit title track from this, her chart-dominating debut. The enigmatic story-song of Billie Joe McAllister's leap from the Tallahatchie Bridge won the Mississippi-born writer-singer three Grammy Awards including Best New Artist, making her the first Country artist to ever win in this category. The Academy of Country Music named Bobbie Gentry its Top New Female Vocalist of 1967.

Ode to Billy Joe reveals Gentry as something of a female counterpart to Louisiana swamp-rocker Tony Joe White. Both specialized in atmospheric Southern tales, wrote their own material and delivered it to funky accompaniment.

Though she never duplicated the success of her debut, Gentry cut a string of Top 10 hits with Capitol Records labelmate Glen Campbell. The best-received was a remake of the Everly Bros. song 'All I Have To Do Is Dream'. In 1976, Gentry's most famous song was made into a motion picture starring Robby Benson. The song 'Ode to Billie Joe' has been covered by many artists including Sinead O'Connor, Tammy Wynette, Ike & Tina Turner, and Patti Smyth with Tom Scott. The song was awarded the Grammy Hall Of Fame Award in 1999.

Number One singles:
US: Ode To Billie Joe

Grammy awards:
Best vocal performance, female – Ode To Billie Joe; Best new artist, Best contemporary female solo vocal performance – Ode To Billie Joe

Label: US & UK: Capitol Records

Recorded in: N/A

Personnel:
Bobbie Gentry
Jimmie Haskell

Producer:
Kelly Gordon

1 Mississippi Delta (3:05)
2 I Saw An Angel Die (2:56)
3 Chickasaw Country Child (2:45)
4 Sunday Best (2:50)
5 Niki Hoeky (2:45)
6 Papa Won't Let Me Go To Town With You (2:30)
7 Bugs (2:05)
8 Hurry, Tuesday Child (4:52)
9 Lazy Willie (2:36)
10 Ode To Billie Joe (4:15)

Total album length: 31 minutes

Bobbie Gentry

BOBBIE GENTRY
ODE TO BILLIE JOE

Capitol RECORDS

EMI

Sleeve artwork by Ed Simpson

85 Hair

| • **Album sales:** 500,000 | • **Release date:** April 1968 |

In many ways, 1968 was the year that '60s rock culture went overground. If 1967 had exploded with such genuine expressions of cultural revolt as *San Francisco* and *Sgt. Pepper*, 1968 is when the fallout reached the mass market.

The enormously popular Broadway musical 'Hair' offered the public a dramatized, somewhat sensationalized account of the hippie scene. To be fair, the story and songs of Gerome Ragni, James Rado and Galt McDermott took on uncomfortable but demanding issues (racism, the generation gap, changing sexual mores), but the work was, after all, a stage play – the antithesis of the new culture's largely improvisational style.

Nevertheless, the *Hair* cast album resonated with audiences, staying on Billboard's chart 151 weeks, 13 of those at the top. What's more, the show's contemporary pop-oriented score generated four hit covers in 1969: the Fifth Dimension's 'Aquarius/Let The Sunshine In' (Number One), the Cowsills' 'Hair' (Number Two), Oliver's 'Good Morning, Starshine' and Three Dog Night's 'Easy To Be Hard' (both Number Three). Original cast member Ronnie Dyson scored several pop R&B hits in the 1970s, including '(If You Let Me Make Love To You Then) Why Can't I Touch You?'

Number One singles:
None

Grammy awards: None

Label: US: RCA;
UK: RCA/Victor

Recorded in: New York, USA

Personnel:
Gerome Ragni
James Rado
Diane Keaton
Paul Jabara
Ronnie Dyson
Galt McDermot
Melba Moore

Producers:
Bertrand Castelli
Andy Wiswell

1 Aquarius (2:54)
2 Donna (2:15)
3 Hashish (0:58)
4 Sodomy (0:55)
5 Coloured Spade (1:12)
6 Manchester England (1:20)
7 I'm Black (0:27)
8 Ain't Got No (0:45)
9 I Believe In Love (1:07)
10 Ain't Got No (Reprise) (1:16)
11 Air (1:30)
12 Initials (0:56)
13 I Got Life (3:08)
14 Going Down (2:21)
15 Hair (3:01)
16 My Conviction (1:41)
17 Easy To Be Hard (2:40)
18 Don't Put It Down (2:03)
19 Frank Mills (2:09)
20 Be-In (3:08)
21 Where Do I Go? (2:42)
22 Electric Blues (2:35)
23 Manchester England (Reprise) (0:32)
24 Black Boys (1:10)
25 White Boys (2:29)

Total album length: 45 minutes

84 Wheels Of Fire

| • **Album sales:** 500,000 | • **Release date:** August 1968 |

In the late 1960s, much effort was made to capture rock bands' live sound, considered superior to studio performances for their energy and spontaneity. Cream's third album, *Wheels Of Fire*, a double LP, offered one live disc, recorded in concert at San Francisco's Fillmore West, and one studio disc.

The latter fares better than the former, and contains some of Cream's most interesting tracks. A Top 10 hit, Jack Bruce's composition 'White Room' is an insistent mid-tempo update of Disraeli Gears' 'Sunshine Of Your Love', while another Bruce tune, the psychedelic-symphonic 'Deserted Cities Of The Heart', is the occasion for one of Clapton's most searing solos. A cover of Albert King's 'Born Under A Bad Sign' plays clean and tough, and the pop piece 'Anyone For Tennis', used in the biker film *The Savage Seven*, provides a pleasant change of pace.

Clapton's driving version of Robert Johnson's 'Crossroads', a Top 30 single, is the highlight of *Wheels'* live disc. Fans and detractors are probably both right about Cream's 17-minute cover of Howlin' Wolf's 'Spoonful' – its improvisations are impressive, for a while.

Three months after the album's release, Cream played their farewell concert. Clapton went on to form supergroup Blind Faith with Stevie Winwood.

Number One singles: None	**Personnel:** Eric Clapton Jack Bruce
Grammy awards: None	Ginger Baker Felix Pappalardi
Label: US: Atco; UK: Polydor	
Recorded in: California, USA	**Producer:** Robert Stigwood Steve Hoffman

1 White Room (4:56)
2 Sitting On Top Of The World (4:56)
3 Passing The Time (4:31)
4 As You Said (4:19)
5 Pressed Rat And Warthog (3:13)
6 Politician (4:11)
7 Those Were The Days (2:52)
8 Born Under A Bad Sign (3:08)
9 Deserted Cities Of The Heart (4:36)
10 Crossroads (4:13)
11 Spoonful (16:44)
12 Traintime (6:52)
13 Toad (15:53)

Total album length: 80 minutes

Cream

CREAM

WHEELS OF FIRE

WHEELS OF FIRE

CREAM

Polydor

Sleeve artwork by Martin Sharp and Stanislaw Zagorski

83 T.C.B.

| • **Album sales:** 500,000 | • **Release date:** June 1969 |

This US Number One album was recorded as soundtrack to a 1968 Supremes and Temptations television special. Because of network programers' need to satisfy a broad audience (including the groups' conventional Top 40 radio listeners and the older television viewers), the album's repertoire encompasses both R&B and traditional pop standards.

In fairness, The Supremes and The Temptations both give rousing performances, but there is a slight contextual dissonance as the flow of pop hits like 'You Keep Me Hangin' On' and '(I Know) I'm Losing You' is interrupted by show tunes and medleys.

Perhaps the record's best moment is the

Temptations' '(I Know) I'm Losing You', which retains much of its grit and toughness despite the big-band arrangements. Slicker by far are The Supremes' medley of 'Come See About Me', 'My World Is Empty Without You' and 'Baby Love' and the program-closing performance of 'The Impossible Dream' from the 1965 Broadway musical 'Man of La Mancha'.

1 **T.C.B.** (2:55)
2 **Stop! In The Name Of Love** (1:12)
3 **Introduction of Diana Ross and The Supremes** (0:55)
4 **You Keep Me Hangin' On** (1:48)
5 **Introduction Of The Temptations: Get Ready** (2:34)
6 **The Way You Do The Things You Do** (3:23)
7 **Medley: A Taste Of Honey/ Eleanor Rigby/ Do You Know The Way To San Jose/ Mrs Robinson** (5:15)
8 **Respect** (2:38)
9 **Somewhere** (3:08)
10 **Ain't Too Proud To Beg** (2:05)
11 **Introduction Of The Temptations** (0:45)
12 **Hello Young Lovers** (2:17)
13 **For Once In My Life** (3:43)
14 **I Know I'm Losing You** (3:07)
15 **Medley: With A Song In My Heart/ Come See About Me/ My World Is Empty Without You/ Baby Love / I Hear A Symphony** (2:47)
16 **The Impossible Dream** (3:10)

Total album length: 42 minutes

Number One singles:	**Personnel:**
None	Diana Ross
	Florence Ballard (d. 1976)
Grammy Awards: None	Mary Wilson
	Barbara Martin
Label: US: Motown; UK:	Dennis Edwards
Tamla Motown	Melvin Franklin
	Otis Williams
Recorded in: California,	Eldridge Bryant
USA	
	Producer: N/A

THE ORIGINAL SOUND TRACK FROM TCB*

STARRING DIANA ROSS AND THE SUPREMES WITH THE TEMPTATIONS

Tamla Motown

*Takin' Care of Business

Sleeve artwork by Ken Kim and Edward M Broussard

G.I. Blues

| • **Album sales:** 1,000,000 | • **Release date:** December 1960 |

Thankfully, there were actual blues present on this soundtrack to Presley's third motion picture. *G.I. Blues* provided him with his fifth chart-topping album, which held that position for 10 straight weeks in 1960. The film hit Number Two on the top grossing films at the box office when it was released. With the full cooperation of the US military, the film marks Elvis' return from his two-year Army stint.

While Presley soundtracks were starting to bulk up on lightweight filler material, at this point they still offered a few morsels the King could sink his teeth into, such as the excellent 'G.I. Blues'. Despite an arrangement that has the Jordanaires counting off 'hut-two-three-four' behind him, Presley swings this blues shuffle with high spirits. He also adds some grit to 'Shoppin' Around', a bluesy-if-subdued rocker in the mould of 'Too Much' or 'Stuck on You'. 'Doin' the Best I Can' is a doowop ballad reminiscent of Clyde McPhatter or the Platters. Here, the vocal is restrained but moving. The song is from the Doc Pomus-Mort Schuman team, which wrote 'His Latest Flame' and 'Little Sister'.

Less earthy – or defensible – is 'Wooden Heart', adapted from a German folksong. Presley struggles gamely, even singing a verse in German, but tracks like this helped diminish the singer's once sturdy rock 'n' roll reputation.

Number One singles:
UK: Wooden Heart
(US: unreleased)

Grammy awards: None

Label: US & UK: RCA

Recorded in: California, USA

Producer: Don Wardell

Personnel:
Elvis Presley (d. 1977)
Scotty Moore
DJ Fontana
Tiny Timbrell
Neil Matthews
Ray Siegal
Frank Bode
Bernie Mattinson
Dudley Brookes
Jimmie Haskey
The Jordanaires

1 **Tonight Is So Right For Love** (2:14)
2 **What's She Really Like?** (2:17)
3 **Big Boots** (1:31)
4 **Frankfurt Special** (2:58)
5 **Wooden Heart** (2:03)
6 **Shoppin' Around** (2:23)
7 **Pocketful Of Rainbows** (2:35)
8 **G.I. Blues** (2:36)
9 **Doin' The Best I Can** (3:10)
10 **Didja Ever** (2:36)
11 **Blue Suede Shoes** (2:07)

Total album length: 27 minutes

Elvis Presley

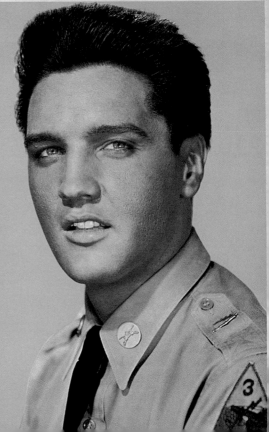
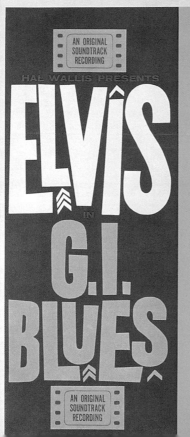

STEREO SF-5078   G. I. BLUES   ELVIS PRESLEY   RCA RECORDS

AN ORIGINAL SOUNDTRACK RECORDING

HAL WALLIS PRESENTS

ELVIS

IN

G. I. BLUES

AN ORIGINAL SOUNDTRACK RECORDING

His Hand In Mine

| **Album sales:** 1,000,000 | **Release date:** May 1961 |

At the end of 1960, following the reissue of his 1958 *Christmas Album*, Presley released the first of several albums of sacred songs. *His Hand In Mine* had a 20-week run on Billboard chart, reaching Number 13. The album was re-released in 1977, when made it to Number Seven on the Country Albums chart.

Four of the album's tunes Presley selected from the repertoire of his favorite gospel quartet, the Statesmen: the ballads 'Known Only To Him' (on which he gives an especially moving performance), 'He Knows Just What I Need', the title track and the medium-tempo 'I Believe In The Man In The Sky'.

The upbeat numbers, particularly 'Working On The Building' and 'Joshua Fit The Battle', lend the album considerable spark, and Presley and the Jordanaires deliver an especially swinging take on 'Swing Low Sweet Chariot'.

While it would be three years before he followed *His Hand iIn Mine* with the album *How Great Thou Art*, Presley recorded three more albums of sacred music between 1967 and his death in 1977.

Number One singles:
None

Grammy awards: None

Label: US & UK: RCA

Recorded in: Nashville, USA

Producer:
Bob Ferguson

Personnel:
Elvis Presley (d. 1977)
Scotty Moore
Hak Garland
DJ Fontana
Murrey Herman
Floyd Cramer
Bob Moore
Homer Randolf
The Jordanaires
Millie Kirkham

1   His Hand In Mine (3:19)
2   I'm Gonna Walk Dem Golden Stairs (1:52)
3   Milky White Way (2:15)
4   My Father's House (2:06)
5   Known Only To Him (2:08)
6   Mansions Over The Hilltop (2:57)
7   I Believe In The Man In The Sky (2:12)
8   If We Never Meet Again (1:59)
9   Working On The Building (1:52)
10 He Knows Just What I Need (2:13)
11 Joshua Fit The Battle (2:41)
12 Swing Low Sweet Chariot (2:34)

Total album length: 28 minutes

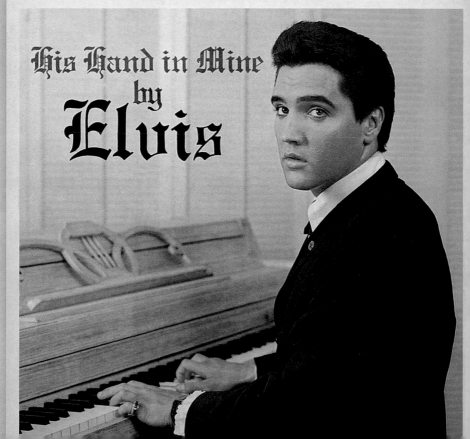

His Hand in Mine
by
Elvis

80

Ramblin' Rose

| • **Album sales:** 1,000,000 | • **Release date:** August 1962 |

Cole had long forsaken his respected jazz-trio career to sing pop by the time he cut *Ramblin' Rose*. Still, a half decade of easy-listening hits was nothing like this. Buoyed by the runaway success of its namesake single, the album remained on the Billboard chart for more than three straight years. With its middle-of-the-road adaptations of country music, *Ramblin' Rose* was a product of its time. The same year (1962) had seen Ray Charles' successful *Modern Sounds in Country & Western Music*, and Dean Martin's string of country-pop singles was less than two years away.

Most of the tracks here frame Cole's rich voice with prominently positioned strings and an unobtrusive chorale. 'I Don't Want It That Way,' a blues shuffle allows Cole some room to shine, and 'The Good Times,' an uncharacteristically (for Cole) pop-R&B item that works off the lick from Leiber & Stoller and Ben E. King's classic 'Stand By Me'.

Cole followed *Ramblin' Rose* with two more hits in 1963, 'Those Lazy-Hazy-Crazy Days of Summer' and 'That Sunday, That Summer'. He died of cancer in 1965.

Number One singles:
None

Grammy awards: None

Label: US & UK: Capitol Records

Recorded in: N/A

Personnel:
Nat King Cole (d. 1965)
Belford Hendricks

Producers:
Lee Gillette

1   Ramblin' Rose
2   The Good Times
3   One Has My Name, The Other Has My Heart
4   Wolverton Mountain
5   He'll Have To Go
6   I Don't Want It That Way
7   Sing Another Song (We'll All Go Home)
8   Goodnight, Irene
9   Skip To My Lou
10 Twilight On The Trail
11 Your Cheatin' Heart
12 When You're Smiling

Official times not available

HIGH FIDELITY

NAT KING COLE
RAMBLIN' ROSE
music conducted by Belford Hendricks

RAMBLIN' ROSE / THE GOOD TIMES / ONE HAS MY NAME THE OTHER HAS MY HEART
WOLVERTON MOUNTAIN / HE'LL HAVE TO GO / I DON'T WANT IT THAT WAY
SING ANOTHER SONG (We'll All Go Home) / GOODNIGHT, IRENE / SKIP TO MY LOU
TWILIGHT ON THE TRAIL / YOUR CHEATIN' HEART / WHEN YOU'RE SMILING

We Wish You A Merry Christmas

| • **Album sales:** 1,000,000 | • **Release date:** October 1962 |

Like the evergreen tree of the season, Conniff's Christmas album was a hearty perennial in the 1960s. Originally released in late 1962, *We Wish You A Merry Christmas* placed high on Billboard's Christmas album chart for the next six years (and into the next decade).

The record was actually the easy-listening bandleader's second holiday set, following 1959's successful *Christmas with Conniff*. Where that LP simply presented 12 classic songs, *We Wish You a Merry Christmas* effectively got more material into its grooves by alternating individual tunes with three-song medleys.

Throughout the album, Conniff's chorale shines, especially on the opening medley's 'Jolly Old St. Nicholas' and 'Let It Snow! Let It Snow! Let It Snow!' from the third medley. The latter is paired with an affecting version of Irving Berlin's 'Count Your Blessings (Instead of Sheep)'. 'Ring Christmas Bells' receives an ambitious arrangement, with the Conniff Singers initially singing rounds then joining for a climactic ending, and in Ray's own words the final medley is 'a masterpiece of performance by the singers'.

Conniff remained one of America's most popular middle-of-the-road artists through the early 1970s, when the genre largely disappeared from the charts. He died in 2003.

Number One singles:
None

Grammy awards: None

Label: US: Columbia;
UK: CBS

Recorded in: N/A

Personnel:
Ray Conniff (d. 2003)
The Ray Conniff Singers

Producers:
Bob Ballard
Ernie Altschuler

1 Medley: Jolly Old St. Nicholas/The Little Drummer Boy
2 Medley: O Holy Night/We Three Kings Of Orient Are/Deck The Halls With Boughs Of Holly
3 Ring Christmas Bells
4 Medley: Let It Snow! Let It Snow! Let It Snow!/Count Your Blessings (Instead Of Sheep)
5 The Twelve Days Of Christmas
6 The First Noel/Hark! The Herald Angels Sing/O Come, All Ye Faithful
7 We Wish You A Merry Christmas

Official times not available

RAY CONNIFF
AND THE RAY CONNIFF SINGERS
WE WISH YOU A MERRY CHRISTMAS

JOLLY OLD ST. NICHOLAS
THE LITTLE DRUMMER BOY
O HOLY NIGHT
WE THREE KINGS OF ORIENT ARE
DECK THE HALL
WITH BOUGHS OF HOLLY
RING CHRISTMAS BELLS
LET IT SNOW!
LET IT SNOW! LET IT SNOW!
COUNT YOUR BLESSINGS
(Instead of Sheep)
THE TWELVE DAYS
OF CHRISTMAS
THE FIRST NOEL
HARK! THE HERALD
ANGELS SING
O COME,
ALL YE FAITHFUL
WE WISH YOU A
MERRY CHRISTMAS

Produced by Rann Productions, Inc.

Bill Cosby Is A Very Funny Fellow. Right!

| • **Album sales:** 1,000,000 | • **Release date:** 1963 |

In 1964, a new comic could not have asked for a better introduction than having his first album produced by Allan Sherman. It speaks well of Cosby that America's favourite song parodist, coming off three Number One comedy albums, was impressed enough by the urbane Philadelphian to do the honours.

Cosby's debut long-player was a Grammy-nominated Top 30 album that stayed on the charts a remarkable two and a half years. Recorded live at New York's Bitter End nightclub, *Bill Cosby Is A Very Funny Fellow. Right!* gave a national audience its first taste of Cosby's keen, kind-hearted brand of observational humour. Cosby's material hits some of the standard 'What if?' subjects of the day ('what if a cop caught

Superman changing costumes in a phone booth?') Other bits are more distinctive, with Cosby enumerating the varieties of entertainment to be found on the New York subway and speculating, over three different routines, how Noah might have responded to God's telling him to build an ark. The latter tracks find Cosby illustrating his story by making his own sound effects, in the manner of his fellow comedian Jonathan Winters.

Cosby was inducted to the TV Hall of Fame, Academy of Television Arts and Sciences in 1992.

Number One singles:	**Personnel:**
None	Bill Cosby
Grammy awards: None	**Producers:**
	Allan Sherman
Label: US & UK: Warner	Roy Silver
Recorded in: New York, USA	

1 **Nut In Every Car** (3:13)
2 **Toss Of The Coin** (2:08)
3 **Little Tiny Hairs** (1:43)
4 **Noah: Right!** (3:32)
5 **Noah: And The Neighbour** (1:11)
6 **Noah: Me And You, Lord** (2:58)
7 **Superman** (0:59)
8 **Hoof And Mouth** (1:43)
9 **Greasy Kid Stuff** (3:04)
10 **Difference Between Men And Woman** (2:11)
11 **Pep Talk** (1:42)
12 **Karate** (5:10)

Total album length: 30 minutes

BILL COSBY
IS A VERY FUNNY FELLOW
RIGHT!

WARNER BROS. RECORDS
1518

LITHOGRAPHED IN CANADA

Produced by ALLAN SHERMAN

Sleeve artwork by Ron Bronstein

77 Little Deuce Coupe

| • **Album sales:** 1,000,000 | • **Release date:** October 1963 |

The Beach Boys were largely a family affair that came together in the Los Angeles suburb of Hawthorne, California, in 1961. Three brothers, Brian, Carl and Dennis Wilson, were joined by their cousin, Mike Love, and a friend, Alan Jardine. One of the undisputed geniuses in popular music, Brian Wilson possessed an uncanny gift for harmonic invention and complex vocal and instrumental arrangements.

The Beach Boys prodigious output offers convincing evidence that the early-1960s pop marketplace was a demanding one. *Little Deuce Coupe* was the group's fourth album in a year. Following three albums on the surfing theme, Capitol Records suggested the band issue an LP of car songs, which were deemed to be more relatable to young consumers out of the coastal zones. *Little Deuce Coupe* collected the previously issued title track (a Top 15 single), '409' and 'Shut Down' and added eight new songs plus a James Dean tribute adapted from a Four Freshmen standard ('A Young Man Is Gone').

The creative chord patterns, vocal arrangements and sparkling production of 'Our Car Club', 'No-Go Showboat' and 'Cherry Cherry Coupe' show that Wilson was entertaining sophisticated musical ideas well before undertaking *Pet Sounds* and *Smile*. The album's success ignited a hot-rod craze in pop in 1963 and 1964, with Jan & Dean and Ronny & The Daytonas scoring Beach Boys-styled hits.

Number One singles:
None

Grammy awards: None

Label: US & UK: Capitol

Recorded in: California, USA

Personnel:
Brian Wilson
Alan Jardine
Carl Wilson (d. 1998)
Dennis Wilson (d. 1983)
Mike Love

Producer:
Brian Wilson

1 Little Deuce Coupe (1:42)
2 Ballad Of Ole' Betsy (2:16)
3 Be True To You School (2:09)
4 Car Crazy Cutie (2:50)
5 Cherry, Cherry Coupe (1:51)
6 409 (1:59)
7 Shut Down (1:52)
8 Spirit Of America (2:25)
9 Our Car Club (2:23)
10 No-Go Showboat (1:56)
11 A Young Man Is Gone (2:18)
12 Custom Machine (1:41)

Total album length: 25 minutes

The Beach Boys

File Under: The Beach Boys • Hot Rod Music • Vocal Group   T 1998

Capitol RECORDS
HIGH FIDELITY

32 LITTLE DEUCE COUPE 32

THE BEACH BOYS

LITTLE DEUCE COUPE • 409 • BALLAD OF OLE' BETSY • SHUT DOWN • OUR CAR CLUB
CHERRY, CHERRY COUPE • SPIRIT OF AMERICA • CUSTOM MACHINE • CAR CRAZY
CUTIE • A YOUNG MAN IS GONE • BE TRUE TO YOUR SCHOOL • NO-GO SHOWBOAT

The Freewheelin' Bob Dylan

| • **Album sales:** 1,000,000 | • **Release date:** November 1963 |

The Freewheelin' Bob Dylan was Dylan's first album to chart, indicating that the attention his songs were beginning to stir up via cover versions by other artists was drawing audiences to the songwriter himself.

The album's relatively successful showing (it charted for 32 weeks, topping out at Number 30) suggests that increasing numbers of people were agreeing with one critic's 1963 assertion that Dylan, born Robert Allen Zimmerman, was 'our finest contemporary folk-song writer'. Ten of *Freewheelin'*'s 13 songs are Dylan originals. These include the early classics 'Blowin' in the Wind' and 'Don't Think Twice, It's All Right',

which swiftly found their way into the repertoire of many of the day's pop singers, jazz bands and easy-listening outfits. Less adaptable but no less inspirational were the songs of political protest.

While a fine interpreter of songs, Dylan was not widely considered a beautiful singer, and many of his songs first reached the public through versions by other artists. Joan Baez, a friend and sometime lover, took it upon herself to record a great deal of his early material, as did others including The Byrds, Sonny and Cher, The Hollies, Manfred Mann and Herman's Hermits.

Number One singles:
None

Grammy awards: None

Label: US: Columbia;
UK: CBS

Recorded in: New York,
USA

Personnel:
Bob Dylan
Bruce Langhorne
Dick Wellstood
Gene Ramey
George Barnes
Herb Lovelle
Howard Collins
Leonard Gaskin

Producer:
John Hammond, Sr.

1 **Blowin' In The Wind** (2:49)
2 **Girl From The North Country** (3:23)
3 **Masters Of War** (4:38)
4 **Down The Highway** (3:32)
5 **Bob Dylan's Blues** (2:28)
6 **A Hard Rain's A-Gonna Fall** (6:53)
7 **Don't Think Twice, It's All Right** (3:40)
8 **Bob Dylan's Dream** (5:02)
9 **Oxford Town** (1:50)
10 **Talkin' World War III Blues** (6:27)
11 **Corrina, Corrina** (2:44)
12 **Honey, Just Allow Me One More Chance** (2:00)
13 **I Shall Be Free** (4:47)

Total album length: 50 minutes

Bob Dylan

THE FREEWHEELIN'
BOB DYLAN

Blowin' In the Wind
Girl From the North Country
Masters of War
Down the Highway
Bob Dylan's Blues
A Hard Rain's A-Gonna Fall

Don't Think Twice, It's All Right
Bob Dylan's Dream
Oxford Town
Talkin' World War III Blues
Corrina, Corrina
Honey, Just Allow Me One More Chance
I Shall Be Free

75

Bringing It All Back Home

| • **Album sales:** 1,000,000 | • **Release date:** March 1965 |

Historically, much has been made of Dylan's 'switch' from acoustic-based folk music to amplified rock. Diehard fans of the former may have booed his concerts, but the greater public could not have viewed it as such a transgression. They made this album, Dylan's first to rely on an electric backing band, his first Top 10 LP and kept it on the charts for nearly a year.

Concurrent with its release, the roiling, rap-like 'Subterranean Homesick Blues' cracked the Top 40. Its walls breached, pop radio became a Dylan-friendly environment. Within weeks of each other, his 'It Ain't Me Babe' and 'All I Really Want

To Do' were turned into hits by, respectively, the Turtles and Cher. The Byrds went to Number One with 'Mr. Tambourine Man' from *Bringing It All Back Home* itself.

The album's more aggressive instrumentation, tunefulness and torrents of imagery revealed still more sides of Dylan. 'Outlaw Blues' is one of Dylan's fiercest rock 'n' roll performances.

Bringing It All Back Home peaked at Number Six on Billboard's Pop Albums chart. The single 'Subterranean Homesick Blues' peaked at Number 39 and Number Six on the Pop Singles and Adult Contemporary charts, respectively.

Number One singles:
None

Grammy awards: None

Label: US: Columbia;
UK: CBS

Recorded in: New York,
USA

Producer:
Tom Wilson

Personnel:
Bob Dylan
Al Gorgoni
Bill Lee
Bobby Gregg
Bruce Langhorne
Frank Owens
Joe Macho
John Boone
John Hammond, Jr.
John Sebastian
Kenny Rankin
Paul Griffin

1 **Subterranean Homesick Blues** (2:21)
2 **She Belongs To Me** (2:47)
3 **Maggie's Farm** (3:54)
4 **Love Minus Zero/No Limit** (2:51)
5 **Outlaw Blues** (3:05)
6 **On The Road Again** (2:35)
7 **Bob Dylan's 115th Dream** (6:30)
8 **Mr Tambourine Man** (5:30)
9 **Gates Of Eden** (5:40)
10 **It's Alright, Ma (I'm Only Bleeding)** (7:29)
11 **It's All Over Now, Baby Blue** (4:12)

Total album length: 47 minutes

Bob Dylan
Bringing It All Back Home

Sleeve artwork by Daniel Kramer

74

Highway 61 Revisited

| • **Album sales:** 1,000,000 | • **Release date:** September 1965 |

It would be hard to overvalue Bob Dylan's importance in 1965. His songwriting had given popular music a new vocabulary, and his unapologetically raw voice had changed notions about singing. As if that weren't enough, he issued his second 'electric' album in less than five months. *Highway 61 Revisited* (titled after the road that led from his native Minnesota to the musical hotbed of New Orleans) peaked at Number Three on Billboard's Pop Albums chart, while the single 'Like a Rolling Stone' peaked at Number Two on the Pop Singles chart.

Dylan delivers ferocious vocals on the breakneck title track, the wonderfully noisy 'From a Buick 6' and the spooky picture-postcard 'Just Like Tom Thumb's Blues'. 'Desolation Row' contains some of his most vivid scene-conjuring, and the lead-off cut, still his biggest 'hit' to date, became a cultural landmark.

'Like A Rolling Stone' was a milestone single when released. Singles were, at the time, never more than three minutes long; it was believed that listeners did not want anything longer. 'Like a Rolling Stone' is six minutes and 13 seconds, and was then and now a huge hit and is often listed as one of the greatest rock and roll songs.

Number One singles:
None

Grammy awards: None

Label: US: Columbia;
UK: CBS

Recorded in: New York,
USA

Producers:
Bob Johnston
Tom Wilson

Personnel:
Bob Dylan
Al Kooper
Bobby Gregg
Charles McCoy
Frank Owens
Harvey Brooks
Hervey Goldstein
Michael Bloomfield
Russ Savakus
Paul Griffin

1 **Like A Rolling Stone** (6:13)
2 **Tombstone Blues** (6:00)
3 **It Takes A Lot To Laugh, It Takes A Train To Cry** (4:09)
4 **From A Buick 6** (3:19)
5 **Ballad Of A Thin Man** (5:58)
6 **Queen Jane Approximately** (5:31)
7 **Highway 61 Revisited** (3:30)
8 **Just Like Tom Thumb's Blues** (5:32)
9 **Desolation Row** (11:22)

Total album length: 52 minutes

CL 2389
COLUMBIA

BOB DYLAN HIGHWAY 61 REVISITED

Sleeve artwork by Daniel Kramer

Out Of Our Heads

| **Album sales:** 1,000,000 | **Release date:** September 1965 |

Their fourth American album, *Out Of Our Heads* was the Stones' first Number One and the first to be recorded mainly in America. In the UK, it was kept from the chart top by *The Sound of Music* soundtrack. It featured their first Number One single, 'Satisfaction'.

While it wouldn't be until 1966's *Aftermath* that the band's albums would consist entirely of original material, *Out Of Our Heads* showcased the best Jagger–Richards co-writes to date. The dynamics of the band began to change, with Jagger and Richards emerging as the leaders of the band. Brian Jones retreated into drug abuse.

The anthemic 'Satisfaction' is joined by the apocalyptic 'Last Time' (a Top 10 single), the saucy blues saga 'The Spider And The Fly' and Play With Fire', whose stark acoustic arrangement revealed new facets of the group emerging as 'the world's greatest rock 'n' roll band'. *Out Of Our Heads* captured the Stones at the most influential point of their early ascent. It's likely that the album was responsible for launching thousands of garage bands.

Number One singles:
US & UK: (I Can't Get No) Satisfaction

Grammy awards: None

Label: US: London; UK: Decca

Recorded in:
Hollywood & Chicago, USA, London, UK

Personnel:
Mick Jagger
Keith Richards
Bill Wyman
Brian Jones (d. 1969)
Charlie Watts
Ian Stewart
Jack Nitzsche
James W. Alexander
Phil Spector

Producer:
Andrew Loog Oldham

US:
1 Mercy, Mercy (2:45)
2 Hitch Hike (2:22)
3 Last Time (3:35)
4 That's How Strong My Love Is (2:23)
5 Good Times (1:57)
6 I'm Alright (2:21)
7 (I Can't Get No) Satisfaction (3:45)
8 Cry To Me (3:08)
9 The Under Assistant West Coast Man (3:08)
10 Play With Fire (2:15)
11 Spider And The Fly (3:30)
12 One More Try (1:58)

Total album length: 33 mins.

UK:
1 She Said Yeah (1:35)
2 Mercy, Mercy (2:46)
3 Hitch Hike (2:26)
4 That's How Strong My Love Is (2:25)
5 Good Times (1:59)
6 Got To Get Away (2:07)
7 Talkin' 'Bout You (2:32)
8 Cry To Me (3:10)
9 Oh Baby (We Got A Good Thing Going On) (2:09)
10 Heart Of Stone (2:51)
11 The Under Assistant West Coast Man (3:07)
12 I'm Free (2:23)

Total album length: 30 mins.

The Rolling Stones

PS 429 **STEREO** ELECTRONICALLY RE-PROCESSED

LONDON

out of
   our heads
**THE ROLLING
STONES***

72

My Name Is Barbra, Two...

| • **Album sales:** 1,000,000 | • **Release date:** October 1965 |

By 1965, Streisand was on an unstoppable roll. The year before, she'd notched her first Number One album and Top Five single, and in April she'd starred in her first television special, 'My Name Is Barbra' for which she won an Emmy. The special also provided part of the material for *My Name Is Barbra, Two...*, the singer's seventh long-player, which followed *My Name Is Barbra* to Number Two. The album went platinum in 1986.

The album-closing medley comes from the TV show, but the rest of the album consists of newly recorded performances. Topping the bill is 'Second Hand Rose'. The campy ragtime tune became a Top 40 hit for Streisand, and the opening ballad, 'He Touched Me', from the Broadway musical *Drat! The Cat!*, was a Hot 100 entry as well. (Both singles made it into the Top 10 of Billboard's Easy Listening chart.) 'The Shadow Of Your Smile' is the main theme from the then-current Elizabeth Taylor/Richard Burton film *The Sandpiper*. The 1959 movie *Porgy and Bess*, which starred Sidney Poitier and Dorothy Dandridge, was the source of 'I Got Plenty Of Nothin', sung here by Streisand to a big brassy Peter Matz arrangement.

Number One singles:
None

Grammy awards: None

Label: US & UK: Columbia

Recorded in: N/A

Personnel:
Barbra Streisand
Don Costa
Peter Matz

Producer:
Robert Mersey

1 He Touched Me (3:10)
2 Shadow Of Your Smile (2:48)
3 Quiet Night (2:26)
4 I Got Plenty O' Nothin' (3:08)
5 How Much Of The Dream Comes True (3:06)
6 Second Hand Rose (2:11)
7 Kind Of Man A Woman Needs (3:55)
8 All That I Want (3:50)
9 Where's The Rainbow? (3:39)
10 No More Songs For Me (2:54)
11 Medley: Second Hand Rose/Give Me The Simple Life/I
   Got Plenty O' Nothin' (5:47)

Total album length: 37 minutes

Barbra Streisand

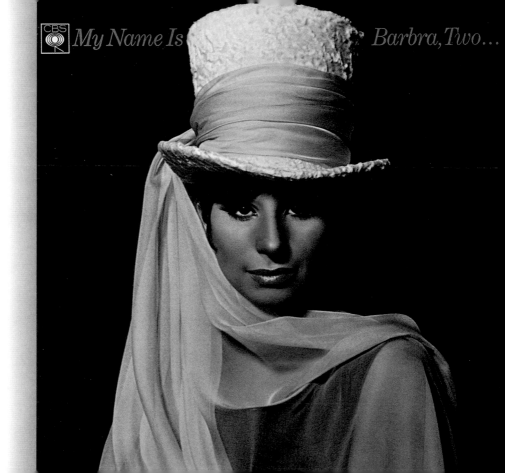

71 Aftermath

| • **Album sales:** 1,000,000 | • **Release date:** April 1966 |

For Stones manager-producer Andrew Loog Oldham, this album was the pay-off for all the effort he spent in 1964 trying to convince Jagger and Richards to begin writing together. The first Rolling Stones album to consist entirely of original material, *Aftermath* helped establish what would come to be one of pop-rock's most formidable composing partnerships.

US and UK versions of the album differ slightly, but the overall effect of both is unified by a lyrical and musical sophistication unheard on prior Stones LPs. The record's varied and creative arrangements owe much to Brian Jones, whose employment of marimbas and dulcimer on cuts like 'Under My Thumb', 'Out of Time' and 'I Am Waiting' add unusual colour and depth. His

sitar work drives 'Paint It Black', a Number One single in both the US and the UK, although only included on the US version of the album.

'Mother's Little Helper', heard only on the UK edition of *Aftermath*, was subsequently released as a single in the US, where it became a Top 10 hit. *Aftermath* was the first Rolling Stones album released in true stereo.

Number One singles: US & UK: Paint It Black

Grammy awards: None

Label: US: London; UK: Decca

Recorded in: California, USA

Personnel:
Mick Jagger
Keith Richards
Brian Jones (d.1969)
Bill Wyman
Jack Nitzsche
Charlie Watts

Producer:
Andrew Loog Oldham

US:
1 Paint It Black (4:30)
2 Stupid Girl (4:19)
3 Lady Jane (3:07)
4 Under My Thumb (3:33)
5 Doncha Bother Me (5:27)
6 Think (6:52)
7 Flight 505 (2:50)
8 High and Dry (4:11)
9 It's Not Easy (7:28)
10 I Am Waiting (3:10)
11 Going Home (11:35)

UK:
1 Mother's Little Helper (2:45)
2 Stupid Girl (2:56)
3 Lady Jane (3:08)
4 Under My Thumb (3:41)
5 Doncha Bother Me (2:41)
6 Goin' Home (11:14)
7 Flight 505 (3:27)
8 High And Dry (3:08)
9 Out Of Time (5:37)
10 It's Not Easy (2:56)
11 I Am Waiting (3:11)
12 Take It Or Leave It (2:47)
13 Think (3:09)
14 What To Do (2:32)

Total album length: 57 minutes

Total album length: 53 minutes

AFTER-MATH

DECCA

70 Wonderfulness

| • **Album sales:** 1,000,000 | • **Release date:** May 1966 |

Wonderfulness was Cosby's best-selling album to date, reaching Billboard's Top 10 and remaining on that chart for well over three years. It won Cosby the 1966 Grammy Award for Best Comedy Performance.

The LP, recorded live at Nevada's Harrah's Lake Tahoe casino, finds the comic in top form, addressing (mostly) his favourite topic: childhood. The set piece is the opener, 'Tonsils', a 15-minute routine about Cosby's bout with tonsilitis. A second extended cut, 'Chicken Heart', covers the young Cosby's affection for things that scared him: 'I had pictures of [Frankenstein, the Wolfman and the Mummy] all over my house. Never looked at 'em!'

At the time, an amiable, apolitical African-American comedian sharing warmheartedly-barbed observations on childhood, parenting, and other rites of passage was a gently revolutionary act. Cosby's effortless ability to address universal experiences transcended boundaries of race and economic class, uniting diverse audiences during one of the most divisive periods in American history.

Although *Wonderfulness* represented Cosby's album-selling peak, he continued to release well-received records, mostly through Warner Bros. (*Revenge, To Russell, My Brother, With Whom I Slept*). His first post-*Wonderfulness* set, though, was 1967's *Silver Throat/ Bill Cosby Sings*, which yielded a Top 10 single in 'Little Ole Man', which adapted the music of Stevie Wonder's 'Uptight (Everything's Alright)' to a Cosby comedy bit.

Number One singles: None

Recorded in: Nevada, USA

Grammy awards: Best comedy performance

Personnel: Bill Cosby

Label: US & UK: Warner Bros.

Producer: Roy Silver

1   Tonsils (15:07)
2   Playground (3:17)
3   Lumps (1:38)
4   Go Carts (5:47)
5   Chicken Heart (12:22)
6   Shop (2:34)
7   Special Class (1:26)
8   Niagara Falls (5:00)

Total album length: 47 minutes

Bill Cosby

STEREO

BILL COSBY
~wonderfulness~

WARNER BROS.
RECORDS
1634

STEREO ● WONDERFULNESS Bill Cosby ● WS 1634

Pet Sounds

| • **Album sales:** 1,000,000 | • **Release date:** May 1966 |

Ten albums' worth of imaginative, commercially solvent rock 'n' roll and nearly 20 Top 40 hits did not prepare anyone for Brian Wilson's masterwork. Despite initial resistance from his label and his bandmates, he persevered – composing (with lyricist Tony Asher), arranging, teaching The Beach Boys their parts and producing the sessions.

Wilson created incredible layers of beautiful harmonies by The Beach Boys, sound effects and unusual instruments like bicycle bells, buzzing organs, harpsichords, flutes, and even dog whistles, on top of conventional keyboards and guitars. In the UK, the album was kept from the top of the charts by The Beatles' *Revolver*. In the US, the album was not as warmly received as previous Beach Boys records, though it generated three Top 40 singles in 'Wouldn't It Be Nice', 'God Only Knows' and 'Sloop John B'.

The complex arrangements of *Pet Sounds* meant that most of its songs never made it into the Beach Boys' concert repertoire. However, in 2003, Wilson, with backing band and orchestra, performed the entire program on selected dates.

Number One singles:
None

Grammy awards: None

Label: US & UK: Capitol

Recorded in: California, USA

Producers:
Brian Wilson
Jim Elliot
Lisa Reddick
Tammy Kizer
Michael Etchart

Personnel:
Brian Wilson
Alan Jardine
Carl Wilson (d. 1998)
Dennis Wilson (d. 1983)
Glen Campbell
Bruce Johnston
Mike Love
Al Casey
Don Randi
Gary Coleman
Various other personnel

1 Wouldn't It Be Nice (2:25)
2 You Still Believe In Me (2:34)
3 That's Not Me (2:30)
4 Don't Talk (Put Your Head On My Shoulder) (2:54)
5 I'm Waiting For The Day (3:06)
6 Let's Go Away For A While (2:21)
7 Sloop John B. (3:00)
8 God Only Knows (2:53)
9 I Know There's An Answer (3:11)
10 Here Today (2:55)
11 I Just Wasn't Made For These Times (3:15)
12 Pet Sounds (2:23)
13 Caroline No (2:53)

Total album length: 36 minutes

The Beach Boys Pet Sounds

Sloop John B./Caroline No
Wouldn't It Be Nice/You Still Believe In Me
That's Not Me/Don't Talk (Put Your Head on My Shoulder)
I'm Waiting For The Day/Let's Go Away For Awhile
God Only Knows/I Know There's An Answer/Here Today
I Just Wasn't Made For These Times/Pet Sounds

Sleeve artwork by George Jerman

68 Strangers In The Night

| • **Album sales:** 1,000,000 | • **Release date:** May 1966 |

His mid-1966 hit with German bandleader Bert Kaempfert's single 'Strangers In The Night' returned Sinatra to the active list of pop music, initiating a string of Top 10 singles. The *Strangers In The Night* album gave Sinatra his first Number One LP since 1960.

The bulk of the album, arranged and conducted by Nelson Riddle, mixes classic and contemporary repertoires evenly. Among the later, the warmly nostalgic 'Summer Wind' gave Sinatra his follow-up hit to 'Strangers In The Night'; the song hit Number One on the Adult Contemporary chart but only Number 25 on Pop Singles. He also sings two tunes by UK writer-producer Tony Hatch. On 'Call Me', he hits an easy stride similar to that of 'Summer Wind'. The more conventional pop standards 'On a Clear Day' and 'My Baby Just Cares For Me' receive more involved performances. Sinatra must've especially liked 'You're Driving Me Crazy', since he kept the take, despite an obvious blown line.

Sinatra followed *Strangers* with two more hits within a year: 'That's Life' and his duet with daughter Nancy, 'Somethin' Stupid', which topped the Hot 100 for four weeks in 1967. He continued recording through the next three decades, scoring hit albums in the 1990s with his Duets albums.

Number One singles:
US: Strangers In The Night

Grammy awards: Record of the year; Best vocal performance, male – Strangers In The Night

Label: US & UK: Reprise

Recorded in: N/A

Personnel:
Frank Sinatra (d. 1998)
Ernie Freeman
Nelson Riddle

Producers:
Jimmy Bowen
Sonny Burke

1 Strangers In The Night (2:25)
2 Summer Wind (2:53)
3 All Or Nothing (3:57)
4 Call Me (3:07)
5 You're Driving Me Crazy! (2:15)
6 On A Clear Day (You Can See Forever) (3:17)
7 My Baby Just Cares For Me (2:30)
8 Downtown (2:14)
9 Yes Sir, That's My Baby (2:08)
10 Most Beautiful Girl In The World (2:24)

Total album length: 29 minutes

Frank Sinatra

Strangers In The Night

arranged and conducted by Nelson Riddle

reprise **Stereo**

reprise 1017

67 Gentle On My Mind

| • **Album sales:** 1,000,000 | • **Release date:** August 1967 |

Between 1967 and 1969, Campbell enjoyed an undisputed reign as America's best-selling male vocalist, holding his own during a period when the charts were almost exclusively dominated by rock bands.

Gentle On My Mind, Campbell's first hit album (he'd issued four previous sets on Capitol), established the template upon which all of his subsequent albums would be modeled. The singer, with producer Al DeLory, selected a comfortable mix of current hits and easy-listening items – with the occasional left-field item thrown in for variation – to which Campbell applied his strong, commercial tenor.

The John Hartford-penned title track was a Top 40 entry on both the Hot 100 and Billboard's country singles chart. Campbell's own composition 'Just Another Man' follows closely in 'Gentle's' footsteps, while 'Mary In The Morning' (a hit by Al Martino in 1967) and Donovan's 'Catch the Wind' tread the folk path to stringed accompaniment. Perhaps Campbell's best moments come in Harry Nilsson's 'Without Her' (one of the first covers of this song) and a sunshine-pop treatment of 'Bowling Green', a 1967 hit for the Everly Brothers.

Campbell's 'Gentle On My Mind' won a Grammy for Best Country & Western Recording.

Number One singles:
None

Grammy awards: Best country & western recording – Gentle On My Mind; Best country & western solo vocal performance, male – Gentle On My Mind

Label: US: Capitol; UK: EMI

Recorded in: N/A

Personnel:
Glen Campbell
Al DeLory
Leon Russell

Producer:
Al DeLory

1 Gentle On My Mind (2:58)
2 Just Another Man (2:12)
3 Mary In The Morning (3:03)
4 Bowling Green (2:20)
5 The World I Used To Know (2:26)
6 It's Over (2:04)
7 Catch The Wind (2:18)
8 Without Her (2:15)
9 You're My World (2:35)
10 Cryin' (2:51)
11 Love Me As Though There's No Tomorrow (2:41)

Total album length: 28 minutes

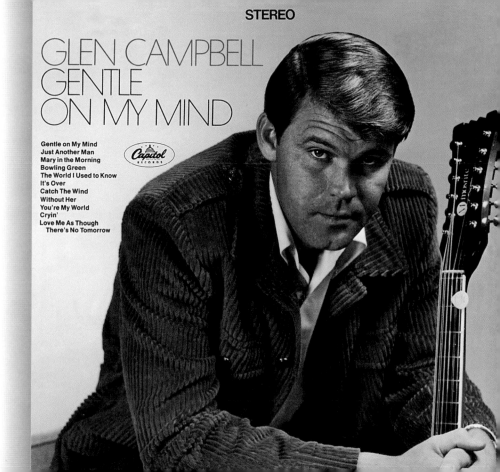

STEREO

GLEN CAMPBELL
GENTLE
ON MY MIND

Gentle on My Mind
Just Another Man
Mary in the Morning
Bowling Green
The World I Used to Know
It's Over
Catch The Wind
Without Her
You're My World
Cryin'
Love Me As Though
    There's No Tomorrow

Capitol
RECORDS

66 Camelot

| • **Album sales:** 1,000,000 | • **Release date:** October 1967 |

Today the word 'Camelot' is generally used to invoke the 'brief shining moment' of John F. Kennedy's presidency, since the musical was a JFK favourite. It's not hard to see why. Camelot was Lerner & Loewe's first score since their mega-hit *My Fair Lady*, and they did themselves proud with a robust and romantic song collection.

Joshua Logan's 1967 film adaptation of the early-'60s stage play was not a great success at the box office (it failed to recoup its then-astronomical $18 million production costs), but its soundtrack clicked both commercially and aesthetically. The album spent 87 weeks on the Billboard chart and earned Oscar nominations for Best Sound and Musical Score, Cinematography and Costume Design.

Vanessa Redgrave (Guenevere) acquits herself admirably on 'The Simple Joys of Maidenhood' and 'The Lusty Month of May,' while Richard Harris (King Arthur) tackles 'How to Handle a Woman' with abundant relish. Harris' best moments, though, come in his reading of the song that so captured JFK, the title tune enumerating the joys of the original 'happiest place on earth.'

A '60s-crooner standard, the touching ballad 'If Ever I Would Leave You' is performed by Franco Nero (Lancelot). Veteran film scorer Alfred Newman handled much of the album's orchestration.

Number One singles: None	**Personnel:** Richard Harris (d. 2002) Vanessa Redgrave Franco Nero David Hemmings (d. 2003)
Grammy awards: None	
Label: US & UK: Warner Bros.	**Producer:** Frederick Loewe
Recorded in: N/A	

1   Overture/Prologue (3:07)
2   I Wonder What The King Is Doing Tonight? (1:58)
3   Simple Joys Of Maidenhead (3:30)
4   Camelot (2:32)
5   C'est Moi (3:54)
6   Lusty Month Of May (3:06)
7   Follow Me (2:55)
8   How To Handle A Woman (3:44)
9   Then You May Take Me To The Fair (4:55)
10 If Ever I Would Leave You (3:29)
11 What Do The Simple Folk Do? (3:41)
12 I Loved You Once In Silence (3:35)
13 Guenevere (5:01)
14 Finale (3:42)

Total album length: 49 minutes

Original Soundtrack

Sleeve artwork by Bob Whitaker and Martin Sharp

64 Days Of Future Passed

| • **Album sales:** 1,000,000 | • **Release date:** November 1967 |

No one would confuse The Moody Blues of 1968 with the British R&B band behind the 1965 hit 'Go Now'. Though three founding members remained, the *Days Of Future Passed* group pursued a loftier musical approach, marrying airy harmonic pop to classical under-pinnings, as exemplified by 'Nights In White Satin', a worldwide smash in 1972.

Deram Records (a Decca imprint) chose The Moody Blues to make an LP in order to promote Deramic Stereo and the group was assigned to make a rock and roll version of Dvorak's 'New World Symphony'. The band convinced the label otherwise and wrote their own album of songs, released as *Days Of Future Passed*. The collaboration between The Moody Blues and conductor Peter Knight's London Festival Orchestra took on a life of its own, ultimately manifesting itself in what flautist Ray Thomas called 'a rock symphony'. 'Forever Afternoon (Tuesday?)', also a single, is a livelier companion of 'Nights In White Satin'. A mid-song tempo shift lends energy to the track, which is otherwise dominated by flute and Mellotron keyboard.

Lyrics like 'I'm looking at myself/ Reflections of my mind' sat well with the lush instrumentation – and with cosmically inclined members of the late-1960s music audience.

Number One singles:
None

Grammy awards: None

Label: US & UK: Deram

Recorded in: London, UK

Personnel:
Justin Hayward
Micheal Pinder
John Lodge
Ray Thomas
Graeme Edge
Peter Knight

Producers:
Tony Clarke
Hugh Mendi

1   The Day Begins (5:50)
2   Dawn: Dawn Is A Feeling (3:48)
3   The Morning: Another Morning (3:56)
4   Lunch Break: Peak Hour (5:33)
5   The Afternoon: Forever Afternoon (Tuesday?)/Time To Get Away (8:23)
6   Evening: The Sunset/Twilight Time (6:34)
7   The Night: Nights In White Satin (7:24)

Total album length: 41 minutes

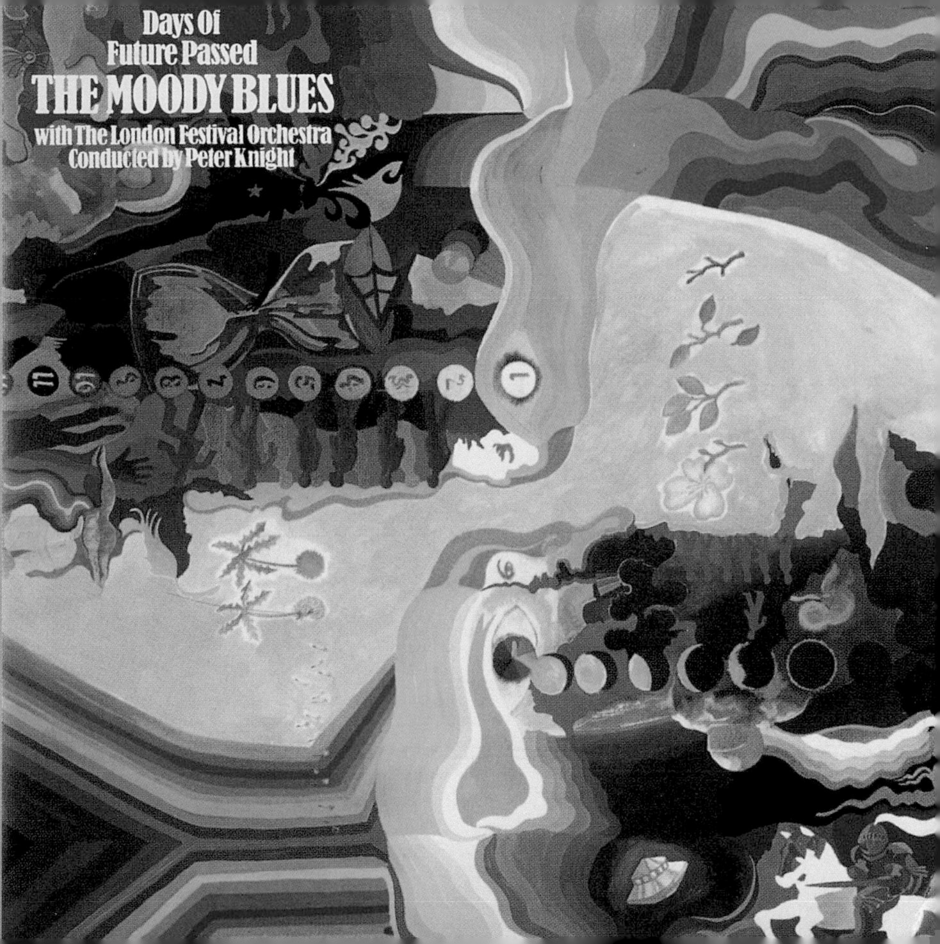

Days Of
Future Passed
THE MOODY BLUES
with The London Festival Orchestra
Conducted by Peter Knight

Sleeve artwork by David Anstey

63 By The Time I Get To Phoenix

| • **Album sales:** 1,000,000 | • **Release date:** November 1967 |

Campbell's follow-up to his successful *Gentle On My Mind* is notable for two reasons. It won the session-guitarist-turned-singer three Grammy awards, most notably 1968's Album of the Year, and it marked the start of his fruitful association with songwriter Jimmy Webb.

Campbell's version of Webb's touching 'By The Time I Get To Phoenix' became a classic of American popular music, though it only reached Billboard's Top 30 (it was, however, a Number Two country single). The song leads off a program that leans more toward pop-country than its folk-flavoured predecessor. The most interesting cut is Campbell's cover of Ernest Tubb's 1945 country hit 'Tomorrow Never

Comes'. He delivers a controlled yet utterly compelling vocal, perfectly pacing the song's building toward a Conway Twitty-styled climax.

Other notable covers include Paul Simon's 'Homeward Bound', Jerry Reed's 'You're Young And You'll Forget' and 'Hey Little One', Dorsey Burnette's soulful 1960 pop hit. The better of two Campbell co-writes, 'Back In The Race' is a spirited, if not so distant, cousin of George Jones' 'The Race Is On'. The folky 'Cold December (In Your Heart)' was written by Limeliters guitarist-vocalist Alex Hassilev.

Number One singles:
None

Grammy Awards: Album of the year; Best vocal performance, male – By the Time I Get To Phoenix; Best contemporary solo vocal performance, male – By the Time I Get To Phoenix

Label: US: Capitol; UK: EMI

Recorded in: Various locations, USA

Personnel:
Glen Cambell

Producer:
Al DeLory

1 **By The Time I Get To Phoenix** (2:44)
2 **Homeward Bound** (2:39)
3 **Tomorrow Never Comes** (2:29)
4 **Cold December (In Your Heart)** (2:29)
5 **My Baby's Gone** (2:52)
6 **Back In The Race** (1:58)
7 **Hey Little One** (2:32)
8 **Bad Seed** (2:20)
9 **I'll Be Lucky Someday** (2:26)
10 **You're Young And You'll Forget** (2:17)
11 **Love Is A Lonesome River** (2:05)

Total album length: 27 minutes

Glen Campbell

GLEN CAMPBELL

By the time I get to Phoenix

62 Strange Days

| • **Album sales:** 1,000,000 | • **Release date:** December 1967 |

The pressure to produce amidst a heavy schedule of concerts, television and personal-appearance dates may have shaped much of The Doors' second album. Released only seven months after the group's debut, *Strange Days* has the feel of an obvious follow-up, a quality it shares with *Magical Mystery Tour*, The Beatle's follow-up to *Sgt. Pepper*, which was released the same month.

Less innovative than its predecessor, *Strange Days* seems relatively benign, relying more on pop-leaning tunes like 'You're Lost, Little Girl', 'My Eyes Have Seen You' and the Top 25 single 'Love Me Two Times'. The rollicking 'People Are Strange' made it to Number 12 on the Hot 100. Innocuous as they are, the pop-rockers represent the album's strengths. Elsewhere, the band perhaps succumbs to the pressure of attempting to match their debut and approaches pretentiousness openly. At 11 minutes, 'When The Music's Over' is an undisguised reprise of 'The End' from The Doors. 'Horse Latitudes' finds Morrison responding positively to press proclamations of him as a poet, declaiming loudly in a minute-and-a-half-long spoken-word passage.

Despite its weaknesses, *Strange Days* sold a million copies, reaching Number Three on Billboard's best-selling albums chart and remaining there for more than a year.

Number One singles:
None

Grammy awards: None

Label: US & UK: Elektra

Recorded in: California, USA

Personnel:
Jim Morrison (d. 1971)
Ray Manzarek
Robbie Krieger
Doug Lubahn
John Densmore

Producer:
Paul Rothchild

1   Strange Days (3:09)
2   You're Lost, Little Girl (3:03)
3   Love Me Two Times (3:16)
4   Unhappy Girl (2:00)
5   Horse Latitudes (1:35)
6   Moonlight Drive (3:04)
7   People Are Strange (2:12)
8   My Eyes Have Seen You (2:29)
9   I Can't See Your Face In My Mind (3:26)
10 When The Music's Over (10:59)

Total album length: 35 minutes

The Doors

42 016
(EKS 74 014)
(stereo)

Sleeve artwork by William S. Harvey and Joel Brodsky

Axis: Bold As Love

| • **Album sales:** 1,000,000 | • **Release date:** October 1967 |

A Top 10 album in the UK and US, Hendrix's second set remained on Billboard's charts just over a year. Its impact may have been less substantial than the previous year's *Are You Experienced?*, but *Axis: Bold As Love* offers more than its share of breathtaking music.

To some degree, the album actually displays more variety than Hendrix's first. There's some precedent for 'Little Wing', but it's a ballad of uniquely delicate beauty, and the supersonic blues 'If 6 Was 9' is a virtual mood ring of shifting space and colour. Psychedelic effects can't disguise the creative musical notions and inventive performing present on such cuts as the majestic title track or 'Spanish Castle Magic', which seems to roar at any volume.

The album was recorded in two weeks at Olympic Studios in London but, disastrously, Hendrix lost the original tapes in a London taxi cab. Back in the studio, the album was re-recorded in another week.

During this period, the band was troubled by increasing personality differences between Hendrix and bassist Noel Redding. These problems, combined with the influence of drugs and alcohol, led to a disastrous 1967–68 tour of Scandinavia and on January 4 1968, Hendrix was jailed by Stockholm police after completely trashing a hotel room. He died in 1970 aged 27.

Number One singles:	Personnel:
None	Jimi Hendrix (d. 1970)
	Mitch Mitchell
Grammy awards: None	Noel Redding (d. 2003)
	Roy Wood
Label: US: Reprise; UK:	Trevor Burton
Polydor	
	Producer:
Recorded in: London, UK	Chas Chandler

1 Experience (1:55)
2 Up From The Skies (2:55)
3 Spanish Castle Magic (3:00)
4 Wait Until Tomorrow (3:00)
5 Ain't No Telling (1:46)
6 Little Wing (2:24)
7 If 6 Was 9 (5:32)
8 You Got Me Floating (2:45)
9 Castles Made Of Sand (2:46)
10 She's So Fine (2:37)
11 One Rainy Wish (3:40)
12 Little Miss Lover (2:20)
13 Bold As Love (4:09)

Total album length: 39 minutes

60 John Wesley Harding

| • **Album sales:** 1,000,000 | • **Release date:** February 1968 |

Following a motorcycle accident and his acclaimed *Blonde On Blonde* album (both 1966), Bob Dylan, born Robert Allen Zimmerman, took an extended hiatus from touring and recording. He returned two years later with the album *John Wesley Harding*. Coming after the *Blonde On Blonde* double LP, this program of short, sparsely accompanied songs prefigured, by a year, the move toward simpler, less 'produced' music-making taken by The Beatles (on the 'white' album), The Rolling Stones (on *Beggars Banquet*) and other groups.

Several of *Harding*'s songs, notably the title track and 'Ballad of Frankie Lee and Judas Priest', are cast as parables. Others, like the romantic 'I'll Be Your Baby Tonight' and 'Down Along the Cove', are image- and irony-free precursors of the straight-ahead country style Dylan would adopt on his next album, *Nashville Skyline*. But it's 'All Along the Watchtower' that grabs the ear. One of Dylan's most enduring compositions, its ominous 'story', told in elliptical, endlessly fascinating verses, seems to anticipate an apocalypse. The point was not lost on the pop-music audience, who made Jimi Hendrix's foreboding version of 'Watchtower' a Top 20 hit in the turbulent year of 1968.

Number One singles:
None

Grammy awards: None

Label: US: Columbia;
UK: CBS

Recorded in: New York
USA

Personnel:
Bob Dylan
Pete Drake
Charlie McCoy
Kenneth A. Buttrey

Producer:
Bob Johnston

1   John Wesley Harding (2:58)
2   As I Went Out One Morning (2:49)
3   I Dreamed I Saw St Augustine (3:53)
4   All Along The Watchtower (2:31)
5   Ballad Of Frankie Lee And Judas Priest (5:35)
6   Drifter's Escape (2:52)
7   Dear Landlord (3:16)
8   I Am A Lonesome Hobo (3:19)
9   I Pity The Poor Immigrant (4:12)
10 Wicked Messenger (2:02)
11 Down Along The Cove (2:23)
12 I'll Be Your Baby Tonight (2:34)

Total album length: 38 minutes

Bob Dylan

STEREO
CS 9604

CL 2804

COLUMBIA

BOB DYLAN
JOHN WESLEY HARDING

59 The Birds, The Bees & The Monkees

| • **Album sales:** 1,000,000 | • **Release date:** May 1968 |

The year 1968 was not a good one for The Monkees. Their television series was cancelled, their movie, *Head*, would fail at the box office, and in December Peter Tork left the group. But things had started off well enough. *The Birds, The Bees & The Monkees* was another successful album, yielding the group's sixth million-selling single in 'Valleri' and yet another Number One in 'Daydream Believer', a perfect, bittersweet pop song from the pen of former Kingston Trio member John Stewart. Both tracks stand out as Davy Jones' finest with the group.

Jones also does lead-vocal chores on 'The Poster', apparently inspired by the kind of circus advertisement that led the Beatles to write 'Being For the Benefit of Mr. Kite,' Carole Bayer's ballad 'We Were Made For Each Other' and the set opener, 'Dream World.' Of four Nesmith songs that grace the album, 'Writing Wrongs' is the most adventurous. 'Tapioca Tundra,' another tune by Michael Nesmith, was The Monkees' penultimate Top 40 single.

The Monkees enjoyed one more album success in 1969's *Instant Replay,* but disbanded in 1970. They have periodically reconvened for tours and album projects.

Number One singles:
US: Daydream Believer

Grammy awards: None

Label: US: Colgems;
UK: RCA Victor

Recorded in: Hollywood, USA

Personnel:
Michael Nesmith
Micky Dolenz
Peter Tork

Davy Jones
Al Hendrickson
Bill Lewis
Don McGinnis
Hal Blaine
Jack Nimitz
Sam Freed
Stephen Stills
And Various

Producers:
Chip Douglas
The Monkees

1 **Dream World (3:16)**
2 **Auntie's Municipal Court (3:55)**
3 **We Were Made For Each Other (2:24)**
4 **Tapioca Tundra (3:03)**
5 **Daydream Believer (2:58)**
6 **Writing Wrongs (5:06)**
7 **I'll Be Back Up On My Feet (2:16)**
8 **Poster (2:21)**
9 **P.O. Box 9847 (3:16)**
10 **Magnolis Simms (3:48)**
11 **Valleri (2:15)**
12 **Zor And Zam (2:10)**

Total album length: 37 minutes

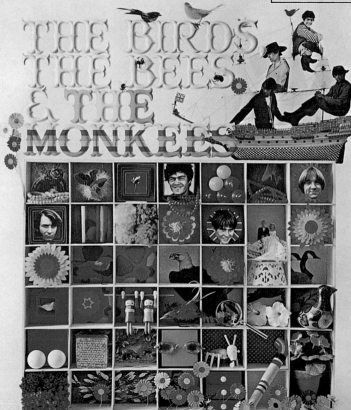

RCA VICTOR · RCA

THE BIRDS THE BEES & THE MONKEES

Funny Girl

| • **Album sales:** 1,000,000 | • **Release date:** August 1968 |

The movie adaptation of *Funny Girl* was not the first time Streisand had played Vaudeville legend Fanny Brice – the 1964 Broadway version of the musical had given the young Streisand her first starring role. Four years later she reprised the role for her film debut.

The movie, directed by William Wyler with musical numbers by Herbert Ross, was an outstanding success. It was nominated for eight Academy Awards, including Best Picture, and won Streisand the Best Actress award. Despite the presence of Omar Shariff as Fanny's husband, the gambler Nicky Arnstein, the film is very much a Streisand vehicle. As the ugly duckling Fanny, she sings on all of the Jules Styne/Bob Merrill tracks except for the 'Overture', the 'Finale' and 'If A Girl Isn't Pretty'.

In many ways the 1968 soundtrack album failed to match the success of the 1964 cast recording. It peaked at Number 12 on the album charts (compared to Number Two for the Broadway version) and the singles 'Funny Girl' and 'Don't Rain On My Parade' never bettered the Top-Ten placing of Streisand's 1964 single 'People'. Nonetheless, the soundtrack has since outsold the Broadway album, earning a platinum award.

Number One singles: None	**Personnel:** Barbra Streisand Omar Shariff
Grammy awards: None	Kay Medford Walter Pidgeon Anne Francis
Label: US & UK: Columbia	Walter Scharf
Recorded in: Los Angeles, USA	**Producer:** Jack Gold

1 **Overture** (4:00)
2 **I'm The Greatest Star** (4:07)
3 **If A Girl Isn't Pretty** (2:27)
4 **Roller Skate Rag** (2:00)
5 **I'd Rather Be Blue Over You (Than Happy With Somebody Else)** (2:37)
6 **His Love Makes Me Beautiful** (5:39)
7 **People** (5:02)
8 **You Are Woman, I Am Man** (4:23)
9 **Don't Rain On My Parade** (2:44)
10 **Sadie, Sadie** (4:19)
11 **Swan** (2:50)
12 **Funny Girl** (2:44)
13 **My Man** (2:11)
14 **Finale** (2:20)

Total album length: 47 minutes

Original Soundtrack

70044

COLUMBIA PICTURES and RASTAR PRODUCTIONS present
the WILLIAM WYLER–RAY STARK Production

FUNNY GIRL

BARBRA STREISAND

OMAR SHARIF

Waiting For The Sun

| • **Album sales:** 1,000,000 | • **Release date:** September 1968 |

Considered against the consistency of the band's first two albums, *Waiting For The Sun* hardly suggests itself as The Doors' best-selling album. It was, however, their only Number One LP.

'Hello, I Love You', the Kinks-derived album opener, was also The Doors' second and final US Number One single and reached Number 15 in the UK. The commercial-pop track seems slightly at odds with much of the rest of the album, whose material ranges from the multi-textured, flamenco-infused 'Spanish Caravan' to 'Not To Touch The Earth', a poetic piece that was to have been part of Morrison's longer, as-then-unreleased 'Celebration Of The Lizard'. There were also political songs. 'The Unknown Soldier',

with its strong anti-war sentiment, stirred some controversy; in the video for the song, Morrison is shown being shot. 'Unknown Soldier' was *Waiting For The Sun*'s only other charting single, making a respectable Hot 100 showing.

Also political, though less respectable, is the album closer, 'Five to One'. Overestimating the strength of the youth (the title refers to late-1960s statistics indicating that one in five Americans was under 25), Morrison warns the older generation to watch its step. 'They've got the guns, but we got the numbers', he sings. 'Gonna win, yeah, we're taking over.'

Number One singles:
US: Hello I Love You

Grammy awards: None

Label: US & UK: Elektra

Recorded in: N/A

Personnel:
Jim Morrison (d. 1971)
Ray Manzarek
Robbie Krieger
John Densmore
Doug Lubahn
Kerry Magness
Leroy Vinnegar

Producer:
Paul Rothchild

1　Hello, I Love You (2:22)
2　Love Street (3:06)
3　Not To Touch The Earth (3:54)
4　Summer's Almost Gone (3:20)
5　Wintertime Love (1:52)
6　The Unknown Soldier (3:10)
7　Spanish Caravan (2:58)
8　My Wild Love (2:50)
9　We Could Be So Good Together (2:20)
10　Yes, The River Flows (2:35)
11　Five To One (4:22)

Total album length: 33 minutes

The Doors

56 Romeo & Juliet

| • **Album sales:** 1,000,000 | • **Release date:** October 1968 |

The score to Italian director Franco Zeffirelli's film of *Romeo & Juliet* was one of the most successful soundtrack albums of the late 1960s. The record remained on Billboard's chart for nearly a year, peaking at Number Two. The score is one of the most popular by the legendary Nino Rota, who composed it after achieving fame with his work on Fellini's *La Dolce Vita* and just prior to doing *The Godfather* and *The Godfather Part II* for Francis Ford Coppola.

The full *Romeo & Juliet* soundtrack was a 114-minute work that included dialogue from the film, as well as Rota's score. The album's best known feature is the piece for the 'Farewell Love Scene.' In 1969, Henry Mancini recorded it, as 'Love Theme From *Romeo & Juliet*', scoring a Number

One record when it was released as a single. (Rota's 'Love Theme From *The Godfather*' was also a Top 40 hit, by Andy Williams, in 1974.)

Nino Rota's later work included scores for Fellini's *Amarcord* and Sergei Bondarchuk's *Waterloo*. Rota died in April 1979.

Number One singles:	**Personnel:**
None	Nino Rota (d. 1979)
	Leonard Whiting
Grammy awards: None	Olivia Hussey
Label: US & UK: Capitol	**Producers:**
	Anthony Havelock-Allan,
Recorded in: N/A	John Brabourne

1 Prologue And Civil Brawl (6:23)
2 How Stand You Disposition To Be Married (9:12)
3 Queen Mab Speech (7:13)
4 Feast At The House Of Capulet (8:48)
5 His Name Is Romeo (2:37)
6 Balcony Scene (9:51)
7 But This I Pray, That Thou Consent To Marry Us Today (5:20)
8 Marriage Arranged (7:00)
9 Tell Me, What Says My Love? (2:42)
10 Romeo And Juliet Are Wed (3:01)
11 In The Mad Blood Stirring (4:10)
12 Death Of Mercutio And Tybalt (11:12)
13 Ascent To Her Chamber, Hence, And Comfort Her (3:29)
14 Farewell Love Scene (4:21)
15 Son, Paris (7:47)
16 Likeness Of Death (2:32)
17 She's Dead, My Lord (6:03)
18 In Capulet's Tomb (10:50)
19 All Are Punish'd (2:06)

Total album length: 114 minutes

Original Soundtrack

Original Soundtrack Recording

PARAMOUNT PICTURES presents
A BHE FILM
The
FRANCO ZEFFIRELLI
Production of
ROMEO
*&***JULIET**

STEREO
PLAYABLE ON STEREO
& MONO PHONOGRAPHS

Capitol
RECORDS

GOLD RECORD
AUDITED AND
CERTIFIED BY
RIAA
AWARD

Leonard Whiting   **Olivia Hussey**
as Romeo   as Juliet

**Dialogue Highlights with Original Score
Composed and Conducted by NINO ROTA**

55 Electric Ladyland

| • **Album sales:** 1,000,000 | • **Release date:** October 1968 |

Hendrix's third album with the original Experience was a US chart-topper and yielded his only hit single, a dazzling interpretation of Bob Dylan's 'All Along the Watchtower', which had appeared a year before on the singer's *John Wesley Harding* album.

A double album, *Electric Ladyland* finds Hendrix with Mitch Mitchell (formerly of Georgie Fame's Blue Flames) on drums and Noel Redding on bass, all doing what they did best. Hendrix wrote most of the original material on the album, although Redding contributed one

track, 'Little Miss Strange'. The sinister live track 'Voodoo Chile' has Stevie Winwood playing organ and Jefferson Airplane's Jack Cassidy on bass. Hendrix's guitar work on the track 'Burning Of The Midnight Lamp' is at once innately lyrical and effortlessly aggressive.

The Jimi Hendrix Experience splintered apart the following year, though Hendrix would release a new album, *Band of Gypsys*, with drummer-singer Buddy Miles, in the spring of 1970. Hendrix died of a drug overdose that November, aged just 27.

Number One singles:
None

Grammy awards: None

Label: US: Reprise;
UK: Track

Recorded in: New York,
USA & London, UK

Producers:
Jimi Hendrix
Chas Chadler

Personnel:
Jimi Hendrix (d. 1970)
Mitch Mitchell
Noel Redding (d. 2003)
Al Kooper
Steve Winwood
Jack Cassidy
Buddy Miles
Chris Wood
Freddie Smith
Mike Finnigan
Larry Faucette

1   And All The Gods Made Love (1:21)
2   (Have You Ever Been To) Electric Ladyland (2:12)
3   Crosstown Traffic (2:25)
4   Voodoo Chile (15:05)
5   Rainy Day, Dream Away (3:43)
6   1983 (A Merman I Should Turn To Be) (13:46)
7   Moon, Turn The Tide... Gently Gently Away (1:01)
8   Little Miss Strange (2:50)
9   Long Hot Summer (3:30)
10 Come On (4:10)
11 Gypsy Eyes (3:46)
12 The Burning Of The Midnight Lamp (3:44)
13 Still Raining, Still Dreaming (4:24)
14 House Burning Down (4:35)
15 All Along The Watchtower (4:01)
16 Voodoo Chile (Slight Return) (5:14)

Total album length: 76 minutes

The Jimi Hendrix Experience

THE JIMI HENDRIX EXPERIENCE ELECTRIC LADYLAND

Beggars Banquet

| • **Album sales:** 1,000,000 | • **Release date:** December 1968 |

The year 1968 found many of rock's best artists getting back to basics after having produced their most ambitious work. It was the year of *John Wesley Harding*, The Beatles' 'white album' and The Rolling Stones' first set since the extravagant *Their Satanic Majesties Request*.

With personal relations between Brian Jones and Keith Richards increasingly frayed, the band returned to the African-American music that had originally inspired them. Despite the tension, and aided by an excellent sound from an up-and-coming producer named Jimmy Miller, Mick Jagger and Richards produced some of their most memorable work on the album – including the distorted, acoustic-guitar-driven 'Street

Fighting Man' and the anthemic 'Sympathy For The Devil' – as the Stones entered the phase that would see them billed as 'The World's Greatest Rock and Roll Band'.

Increasingly Brian Jones was either absent from recording sessions by choice or locked out of them. After his minimal contribution to *Beggar's Banquet,* he found himself forced out in May 1969, replaced by the young, jazz-influenced guitarist, Mick Taylor, then of John Mayall's Bluesbreakers. Within two months, Jones was found drowned in his swimming pool.

Number One singles:
None

Grammy awards: None

Label: US: London;
UK: Decca

Recorded in: London, UK
& Los Angeles, USA

Personnel:
Mick Jagger
Keith Richards
Brian Jones (d. 1969)
Bill Wyman
Charlie Watts
Nicky Hopkins
Rocky Dijon

Producer:
Jimmy Miller

1 **Sympathy For The Devil** (6:18)
2 **No Expectations** (3:56)
3 **Dear Doctor** (3:22)
4 **Parachute Woman** (2:20)
5 **Jigsaw Puzzle** (6:06)
6 **Street Fighting Man** (3:16)
7 **Prodigal Son** (2:52)
8 **Stray Cat Blues** (4:37)
9 **Factory Girl** (2:09)
10 **Salt Of The Earth** (4:47)

Total album length: 40 minutes

Rolling Stones

Beggars Banquet

R.S.V.P.

53 Yellow Submarine

| • **Album sales:** 1,000,000 | • **Release date:** January 1969 |

Yellow Submarine broke a Beatles record. It ended a streak of nine Number One albums that stretched back to 1964, coming in at Number Two on Billboard's album chart. The record's relative failure doesn't reflect poorly on the group, however. *Yellow Submarine* was the soundtrack to an animated feature and contained only four new cuts by the band – all of which had been recorded in the previous two years. The new tracks generally feature nonsense lyrics, befitting their cartoon subject, although Harrison's 'It's All Too Much' waxes philosophical over six minutes of 'Tomorrow Never Knows' styled guitar and tape effects.

The soundtrack also contained The Beatles' previously released title track and 'All You Need Is Love', as well as selections from George Martin's instrumental score. 'Across The Universe' was originally slated for the album, but was scrapped at the last second and instead was put on hold until *Let It Be*.

A newer, re-released version of the album came out in 1999 to accompany the re-release of the film. More recognizable Beatles tracks were placed where the Martin suite originally had been; all of the songs on the 1999 album were remixes prepared for the film's reissue.

Number One singles:
None

Grammy awards: None

Label: US & UK: Apple

Recorded in: London, UK

Personnel:
George Harrison (d. 2001)
John Lennon (d. 1980)
Paul McCartney
Ringo Starr
George Martin

Producer:
George Martin

1 Yellow Submarine (2:42)
2 Only A Northern Song (3:27)
3 All Together Now (2:13)
4 Hey Bulldog (3:14)
5 It's All Too Much (6:28)
6 All You Need Is Love (3:52)
7 Pepperland (2:23)
8 Sea Of Time (3:00)
9 Sea Of Hole (2:20)
10 Sea Of Monsters (3:39)
11 March Of The Meanies (2:22)
12 Pepperland Laid Waste (2:15)
13 Yellow Submarine In Pepperland (2:10)

Total album length: 42 minutes

The Beatles

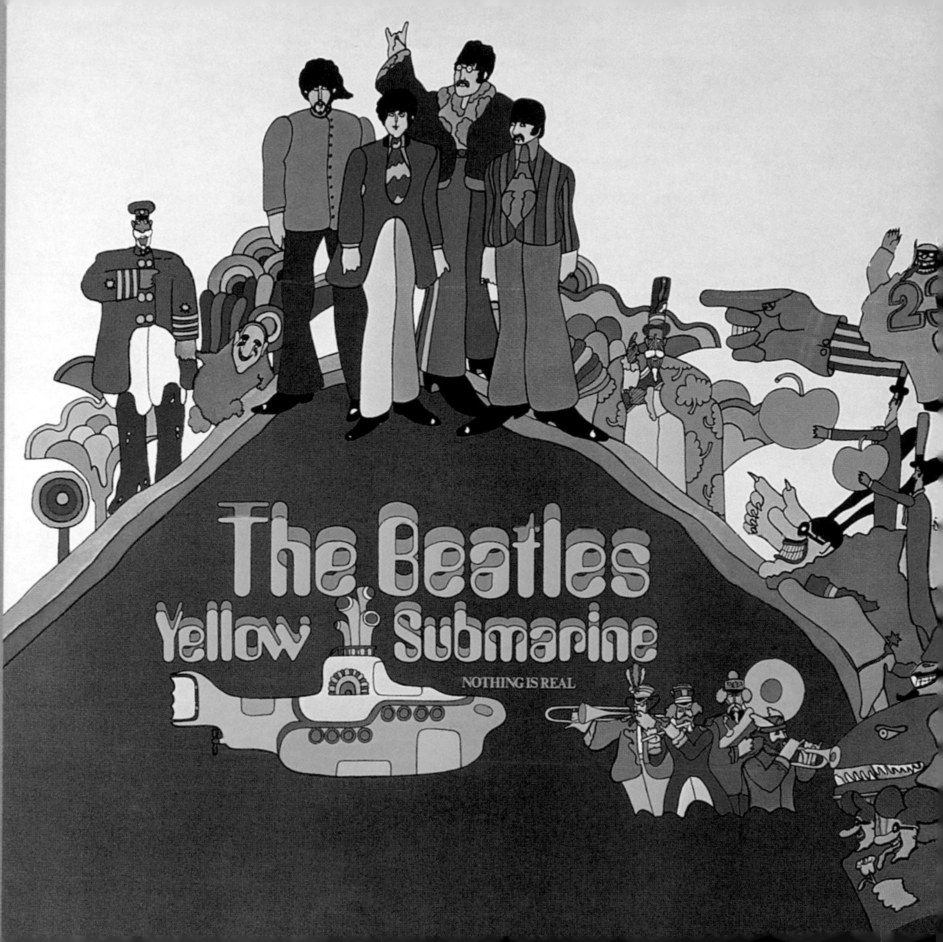
The Beatles
Yellow Submarine
NOTHING IS REAL

52 Galveston

| • **Album sales:** 1,000,000 | • **Release date:** March 1969 |

By the time he released *Galveston*, Campbell had racked up six Top 40 hits and was hosting his own top-rated television series, *The Glen Campbell Goodtime Hour*, which ran from January 1969 until June 1972.

Campbell's third Jimmy Webb-composed single leads off *Galveston*. The away-from-home soldier's tale is the vehicle for one of Campbell's most heartfelt performances, which convincingly and naturally conveys the narrator's conflicting emotions. No less touching is 'Where's The Playground Susie?', another Webb tune that Campbell turned into a hit. Songwriter Buffy Sainte-Marie is the source of two cuts on the album, the ballads 'Take My Hand For a While' and 'Until It's Time For You to Go'. Campbell's straightforward delivery of the latter places it ahead of some of the song's higher-profile covers, including Elvis Presley's.

Campbell's folk-music side is represented by 'Time', a hit for the Pozo-Seco Singers in 1966, and 'Today', Barry McGuire and Randy Sparks' love song that was a hit for their group, the New Christy Minstrels, in 1964. Campbell himself co-authored three *Galveston* tracks, the best being 'Every Time I Itch I Wind Up Scratchin' You', in which a country rambler tries to make amends to his long-suffering wife.

Following the peak period represented by *Galveston*, Campbell continued to enjoy country and pop hits through the 1980s.

Number One singles: None	**Recorded in:** N/A
Grammy awards: None	**Personnel:** Glen Campbell
Label: US: Capitol; UK: Ember	**Producer:** Al DeLory

1 Galveston (2:41)
2 Take My Hand For A While (2:43)
3 If This Is Love (2:10)
4 Today (2:31)
5 Gotta Have Tenderness (2:10)
6 Friends (2:34)
7 Where's The Playground Susie? (2:56)
8 Time (2:45)
9 Until It's Time For You To Go (3:05)
10 Oh What A Woman (2:41)
11 Everytime I Itch I End Up Scratchin' You (1:51)

Total album length: 28 minutes

Glen Campbell
Galveston
Where's The Playground Susie?
GOLD RECORD AWARD
AUDITED AND CERTIFIED BY
RIAA
ember

51 On The Threshold Of A Dream

| • **Album sales:** 1,000,000 | • **Release date:** April 1969 |

The Moody Blues' fourth LP didn't achieve the chart peak of the band's first album in its expansive orchestral mode, *Days of Future Passed,* and it lacked a consensus track like 'Ride My See-Saw' fom the group's second album, but it was still a very popular record. *On The Threshold Of A Dream* was the band's first UK Number One album and reached Number 20 on the Billboard album chart. It remained on the charts for 136 weeks.

On The Threshold Of A Dream somewhat resembles its predecessors, with spoken-word segments and plenty of pretensions. It opens with a recitation of Descartes' 'I think, therefore I am' dictum over a spacy keyboard theme. At its core, the album is a collection of pop-ish tunes pegged to 'mythic' lyrics (Merlin shows up in 'Are You Sitting Comfortably?'). The jangly if mild rocker 'Lovely To See You' and the upbeat 'Dear Diary' are likable enough, and 'Send Me No Wine' effects a vaguely country-ish feeling.

Later the same year the Moody Blues founded their own label, Threshold. *On The Threshold Of A Dream,* was followed by even more popular albums, such as 1970's *A Question of Balance* and 1972's *Seventh Sojourn*. With some personnel changes, The Moody Blues have continued to tour and record.

Number One singles:
None

Grammy awards: None

Label: US & UK: Deram

Recorded in: N/A

Personnel:
Michael Pinder
Justin Hayward
John Lodge
Ray Thomas
Graeme Edge
Pete Jackson

Producer:
Tony Clarke

1 In The Beginning (2:08)
2 Lovely To See You (2:34)
3 Dear Diary (3:56)
4 Send Me No Wine (2:21)
5 To Share Our Love (2:53)
6 So Deep Within You (3:10)
7 Never Comes The Day (4:43)
8 Lazy Day (2:43)
9 Are You Sitting Comfortably? (3:30)
10 The Dream (0:57)
11 Have You Heard (Part 1) (1:28)
12 The Voyage (4:10)
13 Have You Heard (Part 2) (2:26)

Total album length: 39 minutes

The Moody Blues
On The Threshold of a Dream

Sleeve artwork by Phil Travers

Nashville Skyline

| • **Album sales:** 1,000,000 | • **Release date:** May 1969 |

The successor to Dylan's 1968 album *John Wesley Harding* must have seemed even more confounding at the time of its release. Recorded with many of the same musicians, Dylan's ninth album is a country record, built around direct lyrics, hummable melodies and the singer's newly acquired 'crooner' voice.

Nashville Skyline gave Dylan his first Top 10 hit in three years (and his last to date) in 'Lay Lady Lay'. The languorous ballad, originally written for the 1969 film 'Midnight Cowboy' but rejected, has been one of his most popular songs, inspiring pop, R&B and country cover recordings. Another highlight is a reprise of one of Dylan's earliest compositions, 'Girl From The North Country' from the *Freewheelin' Bob Dylan* album, done here as a duet with Johnny Cash. (Country artist Charlie Daniels also guests on the album, contributing guitar and bass.)

The shortest Dylan album (at only 26 minutes), *Nashville Skyline* contains his most carefree, light-hearted songs. These include the word-playing 'Peggy Day', the gentle 'Tonight I'll Be Staying Here With You' and 'Country Pie', whose whimsical verses sound like they could have come from Dylan's *Basement Tapes* experiments.

Number One singles:
None

Grammy awards: None

Label: US: Columbia;
UK: CBS

Recorded in: Nashville, USA

Personnel:
Bob Dylan
Charlie McCoy
Pete Drake
Charlie Daniels
Bob Wilson
Johnny Cash (d. 2003)
Kenneth A. Buttrey

Producer:
Bob Lohnston

1 **Girl From The North Country** (3:41)
2 **Nashville Skyline Rag** (3:12)
3 **To Be Alone With You** (2:05)
4 **I Threw It All Away** (2:23)
5 **Peggy Day** (1:59)
6 **Lay Lady Lay** (3:20)
7 **One More Night** (2:25)
8 **Tell Me It Isn't True** (2:45)
9 **Country Pie** (1:35)
10 **Tonight I'll Be Staying Here With You** (3:23)

Total album length: 26 minutes

Stand!

| • **Album sales:** 1,000,000 | • **Release date:** July 1969 |

The third album by Sly & The Family Stone put the groundbreaking San Francisco septet on the map in a big way. Two certified 1960s anthems came from *Stand!*, the driving 'I Want To Take You Higher' and the Number One single 'Everyday People'.

Stand! displays the group's unique brand of post-Hendrix pop that blends funk, psychedelia and top-notch songwriting. The title cut is a clever call to asserting one's principles ('Stand! You've been sitting much too long/ There's a permanent crease in your right and wrong'). Encouragement and ethics also figure in 'You Can Make It If You Try', which promotes a keep-on-pushin' attitude over a modified James Brown lick. *Stand!* was also notable for its increased political awareness, perhaps best exemplified with 'Don't Call Me Nigger, Whitey'.

Sly & The Family Stone's star rose even higher following *Stand!* and included a triumphant appearance at Woodstock festival later that year and the release of three more successful albums (*There's a Riot Goin' On*, *Fresh* and *Greatest Hits*). The band drifted apart in the mid-1970s, with bassist Graham achieving some fame with Graham Central Station in the 1970s and early 1980s. The band was inducted into the Rock and Roll Hall of Fame in 1993.

Number One singles:
None

Grammy Awards: None

Label: US: Epic;
UK: Direction

Recorded in: N/A

Producer:
Sylvester 'Sly Stone'
  Stewart

Personnel:
Sylvester 'Sly Stone'
  Stewart
Freddie Stewart
Cynthia Robinson
Rose Stone
Larry Graham
Jerry Martini
Greg Errico

1 **Stand!** (3:08)
2 **Don't Call Me Nigger, Whitey** (5:59)
3 **I Want To Take You Higher** (5:22)
4 **Somebody's Watching You** (3:29)
5 **Sing A Simple Song** (3:55)
6 **Everyday People** (2:20)
7 **Sex Machine** (13:48)
8 **You Can Make It If You Try** (3:39)

Total album length: 42 minutes

48 Blind Faith

| • **Album sales:** 1,000,000 | • **Release date:** August 1969 |

Like that other invention of the decade, 'supermodels', 1960s-rock 'supergroups' tended to have short shelf lives. Blind Faith, the much-touted match-up of Cream's Eric Clapton and Ginger Baker with Traffic's Steve Winwood and Family's Rick Grech, produced a Number One album (both in the US.and the UK), but the group disbanded within a year of forming.

What seemed good on paper made for a rather undynamic record. The highlights are clearly Winwood's concise, melodic 'Can't Find My Way Home' and 'Presence Of The Lord', a gospel number that is Clapton's sole compositional contribution. An inoffensive cover of Buddy Holly's 'Well All Right' is included, as well as the undistinguished blues-rocker 'Had to Cry Today', though both cuts find Winwood in good voice. The latter track exhibits Blind Faith's central faults, the late-1960s and early-1970s tendency for musicians to simply carry on too long, in the name of expressing their chops. 'Had to Cry Today' is a minor offence, but the 15-minute 'Do What You Like' is not. The nice enough jazzy groove that kicks off the cut devolves into endless solos. An expanded de-luxe edition of the album was released in 2001 with previously unreleased tracks.

The album's original cover, of a topless pre-teen girl holding a phallic model airplane, was replaced for the record's US issue with a bland shot of the band.

Number One singles:
None

Grammy awards: None

Label: US: RSO;
UK: Polydor

Recorded in: London, UK

Personnel:
Steve Winwood
Eric Clapton
Rick Grech
Ginger Baker

Producers:
Bill Levenson
Jimmy Miller

1 Had To Cry Today (8:48)
2 Can't Find My Way Home (3:16)
3 Well All Right (4:27)
4 Presence Of The Lord (4:50)
5 Sea Of Joy (5:22)
6 Do What You Like (15:18)

Total album length: 42 minutes

Blind Faith

Sleeve artwork by Stanley Miller and Bob Seidemann

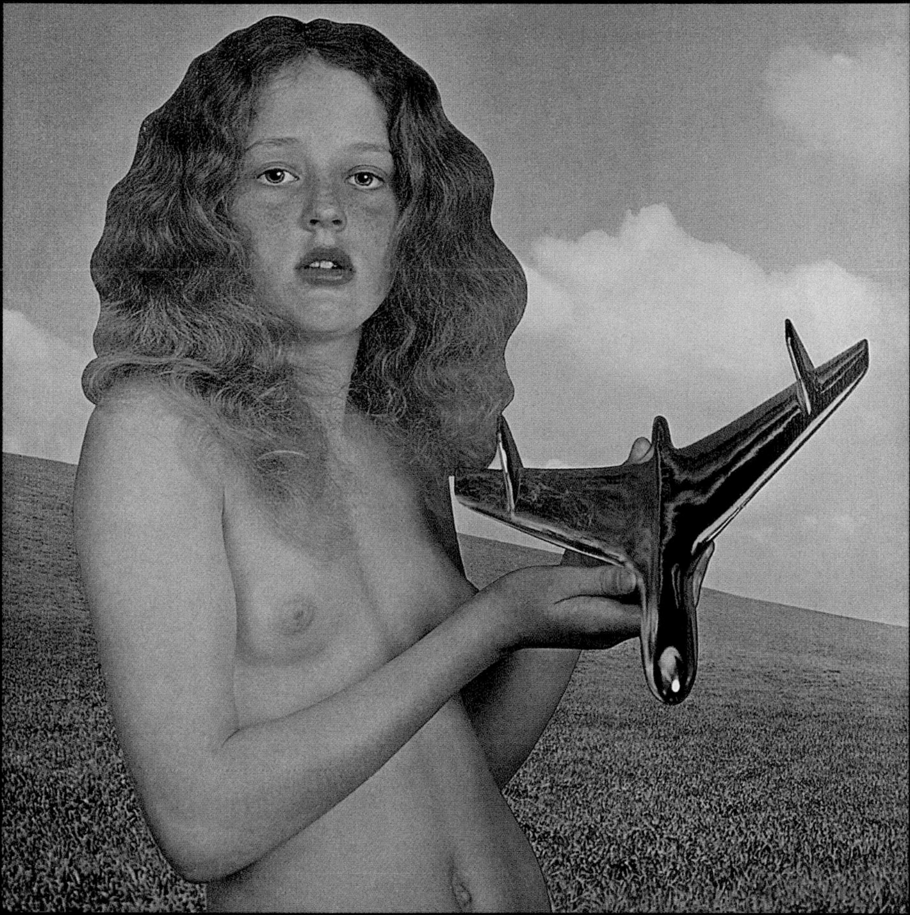

47 The Soft Parade

| • **Album sales:** 1,000,000 | • **Release date:** September 1969 |

Although it went Top 10 in the US, The Doors' fourth album was much less successful – both commercially and aesthetically – than its predecessors and failed to chart in the UK. Weak material appears to have been the culprit. The band augments its instrumental lineup with a profusion of brass, strings and saxes, and it's hard not to see *The Soft Parade* as a collection of arrangements in search of songs.

The strongest cut is 'Touch Me', The Doors' last single smash. It's an ambitious track that successfully stretches the band's usual style and gets a vibrant, at times Sinatra-like performance out of Morrison. During a performance of 'Touch Me' at Miami's Dinner Key Auditorium, Jim Morrison was arrested for exposing himself during the show. He was charged with lewd and lascivious behaviour, indecent behaviour, open profanity and public drunkenness. The three other singles from the album failed to chart strongly: 'Wishful Sinful' reached Number 44 on the US charts, 'Tell All The People' made Number 57, and 'Runnin' Blue' reached Number 64.

Jim Morrison was found dead in his bathtub in a Paris hotel room in July 1971, aged just 27, leaving some fans believing that he faked his death and allowing his legend – as rebel and rock-n-roll poet – to grow ever larger.

Number One singles:
None

Grammy awards: None

Label: US & UK: Elektra

Recorded in: Los Angeles, USA

Personnel:
Jim Morrison (d. 1971)
Ray Manzarek
John Densmore
Robby Kreiger

Harvey Brooks
Doug Lubahn
Curtis Amy
George Bohanan
Champ Webb
Jesse McReynolds
Jimmy Buchanan
Reinol Andino

Producer:
Paul Rothchild

1 Tell All The People (3:24)
2 Touch Me (3:15)
3 Shaman's Blues (4:45)
4 Do It (3:01)
5 Easy Ride (2:35)
6 Wild Child (2:36)
7 Runnin' Blue (2:27)
8 Wishful Sinful (2:56)
13 The Soft Parade (8:40)

Total album length: 34 minutes

The Doors

the doors/the soft parade

Sleeve artwork by William S. Harvey, Joel Brodsky and Paul Harris

46 The Band

| • **Album sales:** 1,000,000 | • **Release date:** September 1969 |

Bob Dylan's four-fifths Canadian former backing group delivered *The Band* a year after its debut, *Music From Big Pink*. *The Band* is an even more cohesive, fine-tuned and accessible set of Americana than its predecessor. Virtually every track on *The Band* is a delight, thanks to the well-written songs and the musicians' jubilant and mournful performances. Although it was never a major hit, the track 'The Night They Drove Old Dixie Down' is a soul-tugging tale of defeat and dignity, and along with 'The Weight' from the Big Pink sessions, remains the song most identified with the group. The song spawned a handful of cover versions, notably Joan Baez' Top-10 version from 1971.

The Band peaked at Number Nine on Billboard's Pop Albums chart. In 2000, it recharted on Billboard's Internet Albums chart, peaking at Number 10. The Band released eight more albums, plus its collaborations with Dylan, *Planet Waves*, *Before the Flood* and *The Basement Tapes*, before disbanding in 1976. The group's final concert is immortalized in Martin Scorsese's 1978 documentary *The Last Waltz*.

Number One singles:
None

Grammy awards: None

Label: US & UK: Capitol

Recorded in: N/A

Personnel:
Jamie Robbie Robertson
Richard Manuel (d. 1986)
Rick Danko (d. 1999)
Garth Hudson
Levon Helm

Producers:
John Simon
Andrew Sandoval
Cheryl Pawelski

1 Across The Great Divide (2:53)
2 Rag Mama Rag (3:04)
3 The Night They Drove Old Dixie Down (3:33)
4 When You Awake (3:13)
5 Up On Cripple Creek (4:34)
6 Whispering Pines (3:58)
7 Jemima Surrender (3:31)
8 Rockin' Chair (3:43)
9 Look Out Cleveland (3:09)
10 Jawbone (4:20)
11 The Unfaithful Servant (4:17)
12 King Harvest (Has Surely Come) (3:39)

Total album length: 44 minutes

THE BAND

Sleeve artwork by Elliott Landy

Peter, Paul And Mary

| • **Album sales:** 2,000,000 | • **Release date:** April 1964 |

Peter, Paul And Mary (Peter Yarrow, Noel Paul Stockey and Mary Travers) launched the most successful folk-music group since the Kingston Trio. Assembled in New York by manager Albert Grossman, the band gradually worked their way onto the lucrative college concert circuit. It was this audience base that sparked initial sales of the album, but it was two single hits that pushed Peter, Paul And Mary to a three-and-a-half-year stay on Billboard's album chart (seven weeks at Number One).

The group's version of Will Holt's tuneful 'Lemon Tree' reached the Top 40 in May of 1962, but it was surpassed, in August, by the rousing 'If I Had A Hammer', which went to Number Ten. Those who looked closely might have sensed a social-political wind shift in this; the fact that Pete Seeger and Lee Hayes' folkie call for justice was sharing chart space with Little Eva's 'Locomotion' and the Four Seasons' 'Sherry' meant times might be changing.

Against the national struggle for civil rights, Peter, Paul And Mary became unofficial early spokesmen for America's younger, increasingly liberal generation. The year after the release of their eponymous debut, they hit the Top 10 again, twice. In 'Blowin' In The Wind' and 'Don't Think Twice, It's All Right' they became the foremost interpreters of Bob Dylan.

Number One singles:
None

Grammy awards: Best performance by a vocal group; Best folk recording

Label: US & UK: Warner

Recorded in: N/A

Personnel:
Mary Travers
Noel Paul Stookey
Peter Yarrow

Producer:
Albert B. Grossman

1 Early In The Morning (1:33)
2 500 Miles (2:46)
3 Sorrow (2:49)
4 This Train (2:03)
5 Bamboo (2:25)
6 It's Raining (4:20)
7 If I Had My Way (2:17)
8 Cruel War (3:26)
9 Lemon Tree (2:52)
10 If I Had A Hammer (2:06)
11 Autumn To May (2:43)
12 Where Have All The Flowers Gone? (3:54)

Total album length: 35 minutes

Peter,
Paul
and
Mary

ARNER BROS.
WB
1449 · HIGH FIDELITY

44 Second Album

| • **Album sales:** 2,000,000 | • **Release date:** April 1964 |

Comprised of selections from various singles and their UK album *With the Beatles*, *Second Album* was the group's second Number One in the US. It was the third of five proper Beatles albums to chart in 1964 and remained on Billboard's chart for one year, spending five weeks at Number One.

The combination of half original songs and half covers makes for what is clearly The Beatles most rock 'n' roll album. McCartney rips up Little Richard's arch-screamer 'Long Tall Sally', while Lennon makes combustible devices of three Motown standards – Barret Strong's 'Money', the Miracles' 'You've Really Got A Hold On Me' and, especially, the Marvelettes' 'Please Mr Postman'. He's in more restrained form on 'Devil In Her

Heart', a cover of the Donays' girl-group song.

Among the Beatle originals, 'She Loves You' is the most prominent, having been the band's second single to top the Hot 100 in America. 'I'll Get You' and 'I Call Your Name' are strong melodic pop-rock entries, but 'You Can't Do That' is even better, showcasing taut, abrasive guitar playing from Harrison, powerful drumming by Ringo and one of Lennon's most commanding vocal workouts.

Number One singles:
US & UK: Can't Buy Me Love

Grammy awards: None

Label: US: Capitol; UK: Parlophone

Recorded in: London, UK

Personnel:
John Lennon (d. 1980)
Paul McCartney
George Harrison (d. 2001)
Ringo Starr
George Martin

Producer:
George Martin

1 Roll Over Beethoven (2:44)
2 Thank You Girl (2:01)
3 You Really Got A Hold On Me (2:58)
4 Devil In Her Heart (2:23)
5 Money (2:47)
6 You Can't Do That (2:23)
7 Long Tall Sally (2:03)
8 I Call Your Name (2:09)
9 Please Mr Postman (2:34)
10 I'll Get You (2:04)
11 She Loves You (2:19)

Total album length: 24 minutes

The Beatles

CAPITOL FULL DIMENSIONAL STEREO

THE BEATLES'
SECOND ALBUM

featuring

SHE LOVES YOU

and

ROLL OVER BEETHOVEN

ELECTRIFYING BIG-BEAT PERFORMANCES BY ENGLAND'S
Paul McCartney, John Lennon, George Harrison and Ringo Starr

Capitol RECORDS

HIGH FIDELITY

43 Fiddler On The Roof

| • **Album sales:** 2,000,000 | • **Release date:** September 1964 |

While it never became a Number One album (it peaked at Number Seven), the cast album from Broadway's *Fiddler on the Roof* remained a fixture on Billboard's album chart for just under four years.

The story of a Jewish man and his three daughters in Russia at the turn of the last century premiered in 1964 and still enjoys frequent revivals around the world. Just as enduring as the play, Jerry Bock and Sheldon Harnick's score

has made a continuing contribution to the American popular songbook. 'Sunrise, Sunset', performed by patriarch Tevye (Zero Mostel) with his family, is the best known of the Fiddler songs. It served as the basis for Easy Listening hits by pianist Roger Williams (1967) and singer Eddie Fisher (1965). Tevye's three daughters team for the sprightly 'Matchmaker'.

While the album generated no pop hits, the songs have found their way into the concert and recorded repertoire of numerous artists, from Ella Fitzgerald to the Four Tops. The show's main theme, heard here under Tevye's prologue and 'Tradition', has also made dozens of album appearances (although it is usually simply listed as 'Fiddler On The Roof').

Number One singles: None

Grammy awards: None

Label: US: RCA Victor; UK: CBS

Recorded in: N/A

Personnel:
Zero Mostel (d. 1977)
Beatrice Arthur
Carol Sawyer
Julia Migenes
Sue Babel
Tanya Everett

Austin Pendleton
Bert Convy
Gluck Sandor
Ross Gifford
Joanna Merlin
Maria Karnilova
Leonard Frey
Michael Granger
Richard Leonard
Vladimir Spivakov
Don Walker

Producers:
Andy Wiswell
Maurice Levine
Jay David Saks
Vincent Caro

1 **Prologue - Tradition** (6:53)
2 **Matchmaker** (3:41)
3 **If I Were A Rich Man** (4:54)
4 **Sabbath Prayer** (2:26)
5 **To Life** (4:11)
6 **Miracles Of Miracles** (2:01)
7 **Dream** (6:07)
8 **Sunrise, Sunset** (3:33)
9 **Wedding Dance** (2:11)
10 **Now I Have Everything** (2:03)
11 **Do You Love Me?** (3:08)
12 **Rumour** (1:52)
13 **Far From The Home I Love** (3:29)
14 **Anatevka** (3:08)

Total album length: 50 minutes

Original Cast Recording

70030

CBS

ORIGINAL LONDON CAST ALBUM

Harold Prince and Richard Pilbrow present

TOPOL

in a new musical

FIDDLER ON THE ROOF

book by
Joseph Stein
based on Sholom Aleichem's stories
by special permission of Arnold Perl

music by
Jerry Bock

lyrics by
Sheldon Harnick

also starring
Miriam Karlin

entire production directed & choreographed by
Jerome Robbins

Topol
in a New Musical
Fiddler on the Roof

42 Yesterday And Today

| • **Album sales:** 2,000,000 | • **Release date:** July 1966 |

Capitol Records' penchant for altering The Beatles original UK output for US consumption reached its zenith with *Yesterday And Today*. By the time of the album's release, the label's whittling down of the group's British albums (to conform to shorter US running times) and grafting on of non-album hit singles had netted Capitol enough surplus material for several US-only LPs.

For this summer 1966 release, Capitol corralled a recent batch of stray tracks, gathering non-album Number Ones ('We Can Work It Out', 'Yesterday'), orphaned album cuts ('Drive My Car', 'If I Needed Someone') and, to flesh out the new disc's program, three new John Lennon songs ('And Your Bird Can Sing', 'Dr Robert' and

'I'm Only Sleeping', with its innovative backwards guitars) hastily pulled from sessions for the upcoming *Revolver* album.

For the album, The Beatles supplied a cover photo of themselves in butcher smocks, covered with slabs of raw meat and baby doll parts. The ensuing uproar forced Capitol to quickly withdraw the controversial cover and replace it with an innocuous shot of four very bored Beatles. The original has since become a highly prized collectable.

Number One singles:
US & UK: Day Tripper

Grammy awards: None

Label: US: Capitol;
UK: Parlophone

Recorded in: N/A

Personnel:
John Lennon (d. 1980)
Paul McCartney
George Harrison (d. 2001)
Ringo Starr

Producer:
George Martin

1 Drive My Car (2:30)
2 I'm Only Sleeping (3:01)
3 Nowhere Man (2:45)
4 Dr Robert (2:15)
5 Yesterday (2:08)
6 Act Naturally (2:33)
7 And Your Bird Can Sing (2:01)
8 If I Need Someone (2:24)
9 We Can Work It Out (2:15)
10 What Goes On (2:51)
11 Day Tripper (2:50)

Total album length: 28 minutes

The Beatles

NEW IMPROVED FULL DIMENSIONAL STEREO

YESTERDAY · DR. ROBERT
I'M ONLY SLEEPING · AND YOUR BIRD CAN SING
WE CAN WORK IT OUT · DAY TRIPPER
NOWHERE MAN · WHAT GOES ON?
DRIVE MY CAR · IF I NEEDED SOMEONE
ACT NATURALLY

The Beatles Yesterday And Today

GOLD RECORD AWARD
AUDITED AND CERTIFIED BY
RIAA

Sleeve artwork by Robert Freeman

41 Blonde On Blonde

| • **Album sales:** 2,000,000 | • **Release date:** May 1966 |

'The closest I ever got to the sound I hear in my head was on individual tracks in the *Blonde On Blonde* album', Dylan has said. 'It's that thin, that wild mercury sound.'

Dylan achieved his ideal on a sprawling double LP recorded with the cream of Nashville's session musicians (and longtime accompanists Al Kooper and Robbie Robertson). The players' professionalism enabled Dylan to concentrate on lyric-writing, much of which he has said occurred in the studio as the musicians took breaks.

Blonde On Blonde is regarded widely as Dylan's masterwork. The powerful music, a combination of blues, traditional country and even martial beats ('Most Likely You'll Go Your Way'), matches the haunting, hallucinogenic imagery to create an utterly unique soundscape. Songs of out-and-out silliness ('Leopard-Skin Pill-Box Hat' and 'Rainy Day Woman No. 12 & 35', a Number Two single) coexist with what is perhaps Dylan's most poignant ballad, the oft-covered 'Just Like A Woman'.

Number One singles:
None

Grammy awards: None

Label: US: Columbia;
UK: CBS

Recorded in: Nashville
and New York, USA

Personnel:
Bob Dylan
Al Kooper
Bill Atkins
Charlie McCoy

Garth Hudson
Hargus 'Pig' Robbins
Henry Strzelecki
Jerry Kennedy
Joe South
Kenneth A. Buttrey
Paul Griffin
Richard Manuel
Rick Danko
Robbie Robertson
Sanford Konikoff
Wayne Butler
Wayne Moss

Producer:
Bob Johnston

1 **Rainy Day Women Nos. 12 & 35** (4:33)
2 **Pledging My Time** (3:42)
3 **Visions Of Johanna** (7:27)
4 **One Of Us Must Know (Sooner Or Later)** (4:53)
5 **Most Likely You Go Your Way (And I'll Go Mine)** (3:22)
6 **Temporary Like Achilles** (5:03)
7 **Absolutely Sweet Marie** (4:46)
8 **4th Time Around** (4:26)
9 **Obviously 5 Believers** (3:30)
10 **I Want You** (3:06)
11 **Stuck inside of Memphis With The Mobile Blues Again** (7:04)
12 **Leopard-Skin Pill-Box Hat** (3:50)
13 **Just Like A Woman** (4:39)
14 **Sad Eyed Lady Of The Lowlands** (11:19)

Total album length: 72 minutes

STEREO
Can Also Be Played in Mono

featuring I WANT YOU and RAINY DAY WOMEN Nos. 12 & 35

Sleeve artwork by Josephine DiDonato

40 The Doors

| • **Album sales:** 2,000,000 | • **Release date:** March 1967 |

Although their music was built from many of the same elements as that of The Rolling Stones, Animals or Yardbirds, The Doors' debut album, recorded at Sunset Sound Recorders in California, announced the arrival of a strikingly original band.

Ray Manzarek's stylish keyboard work and guitarist Robbie Krieger's liquid melody lines transform Willie Dixon's 'Backdoor Man' and similarly blues-based group compositions into something new: seductive, ominous rock, often with pronounced literary aspirations. The pleasure-bent, endlessly covered 'Light My Fire', Number One for three weeks during 1967's Summer of Love, remains an official anthem of the 1960s. The urgency of the age is palpable in 'Break On Through', Jim Morrison's vocal pushing change and transcendence over an imperative organ-drums riff.

The Rolling Stones' 'Goin' Home' and the extended jams of San Francisco's psychedelic bands may have preceded Morrison's 'The End', but the 11-minute Oedipal freakout was still an unprecedented performance. The climax of many early Doors shows, the song played a key role in the rise of Morrison as the prototypical post-Presley rock star: a daring, dangerous, self-described 'erotic politician'. 'The End' was used to open *Apocalypse Now*, Francis Ford Coppola's 1979 film about American soldiers in Vietnam.

Number One singles:
US: Light My Fire

Grammy awards: None

Label: US & UK: Elektra

Recorded in: Hollywood, USA

Personnel:
Jim Morrison (d. 1971)
Ray Manzarek
Robbie Krieger
John Densmore
Larry Knechtel

Producer:
Paul Rothchild

1 Break On Through (To The Other Side) (2:25)
2 Soul Kitchen (3:30)
3 The Crystal Ship (2:30)
4 Twentieth Century Fox (2:30)
5 Alabama Song (Whiskey Song) (3:15)
6 Light My Fire (6:30)
7 Backdoor Man (3:30)
8 I Looked At You (2:18)
9 End Of The Night (2:49)
10 Take It As Comes (2:13)
11 The End (11:35)

Total album length: 43 minutes

The Doors

The doors

42 012
(EKS 74 007)
(stereo)

39 How Great Thou Art

| • **Album sales:** 2,000,000 | • **Release date:** April 1967 |

Few gospel albums have the distinction of having spun off Top 40 singles. Presley's *How Great Thou Art* joined the small circle that includes the Mormon Tabernacle Choir's *The Lord's Prayer* ('Battle Hymn of the Republic', 1959) and the Edwin Hawkins Singers' *Let Us Go Into the House Of The Lord* ('Oh Happy Day', 1969). 'Crying In The Chapel', featured here, had made Number Three on the Hot 100 in 1965 – the track had been recorded five years earlier and held back.

The other selections on the album alternate between devotional ballads ('Where No One Stands Alone') and roof-raising, tambourine-shaking uptempo tunes ('Without Him', 'By and

By'). The midtempo 'Where Could I Go To But the Lord' hits a bluesy, finger-snapping stride. Throughout the album, Presley sounds involved and focused, which was not always the case on his pop albums of this period.

How Great Thou Art was Presley's second gospel album. Some measure of how strongly the singer felt about sacred music is reflected in the fact that, despite a hectic recording schedule, he found time to deliver such albums. This one fell between the soundtracks *Spinout* (October 1966) and *Double Trouble* (June 1967).

Number One singles:
None

Grammy awards: Best
sacred performance; Best
inspirational performance

Label: US & UK: RCA

Recorded in: Nashville,
USA

Personnel:
Elvis Presley (d. 1977)
The Imperials Quartet
The Jordanaires

Producer:
Felton Jarvis

1   How Great Thou Art (3:04)
2   In The Garden (3:13)
3   Without Him (2:32)
4   By And By (1:53)
5   Somebody Bigger Than You Or I (2:30)
6   Stand By Me (2:29)
7   Farther Along (4:07)
8   Where Could I Go To But The Lord (3:39)
9   Crying In The Chapel (2:24)
10 If The Lord Wasn't By My Side (1:40)
11 So High (1:59)
12 Run On (2:24)
13 Where No One Stands Alone (2:44)

Total album length: 35 minutes

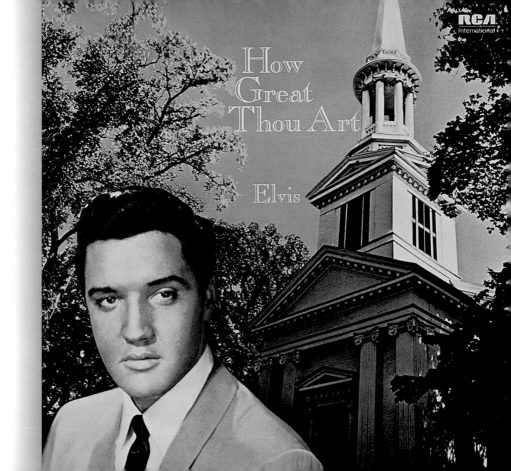

38 Headquarters

| • **Album sales:** 2,000,000 | • **Release date:** June 1967 |

The first album recorded by The Monkees after the acrimonious departure of their music supervisor, Don Kirshner, *Headquarters* is also the first album on which the group members play instruments as well as sing on every track.

Another Number One album, *Headquarters* was released in the summer of 1967, just as the lysergic 'Light My Fire' and 'White Rabbit' were ascending the charts. Whether The Monkees were responding to the tenor of the times or merely following their own instincts, *Headquarters* comes across a less sunny, more pensive album than their previous offerings.

Peter Tork's 'For Pete's Sake' was adopted as the closing theme for The Monkees' television series. Dolenz's 'Randy Scouse Git' touches such stylistic bases as ragtime and protest and was composed in London, following a party thrown for The Monkees by The Beatles. Unfortunately for The Monkees, *Headquarters* was released only shortly before *Sgt Pepper*, and was displaced after only a week at Number One.

The Monkees also deserve credit for helping bring American attention to the Jimi Hendrix Experience, who they asked for as an opening act during a 1967 concert tour.

Number One singles:
None

Grammy Awards: None

Label: US: Colgems;
UK: RCA Victor

Recorded in:
California, USA

Personnel:
Michael Nesmith
Micky Dolenz
Peter Tork
Davy Jones
Frederick Seykora
Jerry Yester
Keith Allison
Vincent DaRosa

Producers:
Chip Douglas
Douglas Farthing-Hatfield

1 You Told Me (2:22)
2 I'll Spend My Life With You (2:23)
3 Forget That Girl (2:21)
4 Band 6 (0:38)
5 You Just May Be The One (2:00)
6 Shades Of Grey (3:20)
7 I Can't Get Her Off My Mind (2:23)
8 For Pete's Sake (2:10)
9 Mr. Webster (2:02)
10 Sunny Girlfriend (2:31)
11 Zilch (1:05)
12 No Time (2:09)
13 Early Morning Blues And Greens (2:00)
14 Randy Scouse Git (2:35)

Total album length: 30 minutes

The Monkees

mono RD-7886

RCA VICTOR ® RCA ®

THE MONKEES HEADQUARTERS

37 Pisces, Aquarius, Capricorn & Jones Ltd.

| • **Album sales:** 2,000,000 | • **Release date:** January 1968 |

On their fourth album, the group rebounded with a strong collection that garnered a fourth (and final) Number One album and two significant hit singles.

If Gerry Goffin and Carole King's critique of suburban values, 'Pleasant Valley Sunday', seemed somewhat quaint, coming as it did two years after the heyday of social-protest rock, it's the basis for what is arguably The Monkees' best three minutes. The album's other hit, Boyce & Hart's moody garage-rocker 'Words', benefits from Dolenz's multi-tracked vocals. Harry

Nilsson's 'Cuddly Toy' provides a suitable sunshine-pop vehicle for Jones, who also takes on Jeff Barry's suggestive 'She Hangs Out' and Goffin-King's knowing sketch of the groupie world, 'Star Collector'.

Such subject matter indicated The Monkees knew that their audience, like the rest of its generation, was maturing. Following the peak of the album's chart run, the group commenced filming of its feature film, *Head*, written by Bob Rafelson and starring Jack Nicholson. The film featured cameos of, among others, such countercultural figures as Frank Zappa.

Number One singles: None

Grammy awards: None

Label: US: Colgems; UK: RCA Victor

Recorded in: Hollywood, New York & Nashville, USA

Personnel:
Mike Nesmith
Micky Dolenz
Peter Tork
Davy Jones
Chip Douglas
Bill Martin
Paul Beaver
Bob Rafelson
Various other personnel

Producers:
Chip Douglas
Faithling Hatfield
Bill Inglot
Harold Bronson

1 Salesman (2:03)
2 She Hangs Out (2:33)
3 The Door Into Summer (2:50)
4 Love Is Only Sleeping (2:28)
5 Cuddly Toy (2:45)
6 Words (2:48)
7 Hard To Believe (2:33)
8 What Am I Doing Hangin' 'Round (3:02)
9 Peter Perceval Patterson's Pet Pig Porky (00:17)
10 Pleasant Valley Sunday (3:13)
11 Daily Nightly (2:26)
12 Don't Call On Me (2:28)
13 Star Collector (3:30)

Total album length: 33 minutes

RD-7912

RCA VICTOR

PISCES, AQUARIUS, CAPRICORN & JONES LTD.

MONKEES

36 Bookends

| • **Album sales:** 2,000,000 | • **Release date:** July 1968 |

While it features two of Paul Simon's best whimsical-pop songs in 'Punky's Dilemma' and 'At The Zoo' (a Top 20 single), at its heart *Bookends* addresses deeper, darker concerns. Released in a year that saw increased escalation of the Vietnam War, riots at Chicago's Democratic convention and the assassinations of Martin Luther King and Robert Kennedy, *Bookends* characterizes the more thoughtful turn much of pop was taking in 1968.

Astonishingly mature songs to have come from the pen of a 26-year-old, Simon's 'America' and 'Old Friends' acknowledge the need to seek comfort and consolation in a world grown more personally and socially confusing. Even less sunnily disposed are the self-accusatory 'Fakin'

It' and 'A Hazy Shade Of Winter', which urges action in the face of rapidly diminishing possibilities. Both tracks were Top 30 singles; in 1988, The Bangles reached Number Two with a cover of the latter song.

Bookends was a more 'produced' record than previous Simon & Garfunkel sets. While tastefully applied, such post-*Sgt. Pepper* devices as an establishing instrumental theme, sound collages and audio verite bits inserted into songs mark the album as a product of its time. It topped the charts in the US for seven weeks and in the UK for five weeks.

Number One singles:
US: Mrs Robinson

Grammy awards: None

Label: US: Columbia;
UK: CBS

Recorded in: N/A

Personnel:
Art Garfunkel
Paul Simon

Producers:
Art Garfunkel
Paul Simon
Bob Johnston
Roy Halee

1 Bookends Theme (0:32)
2 Save The Life Of My Child (2:48)
3 America (3:35)
4 Overs (2:18)
5 Voices Of Old People (2:07)
6 Old Friends (4:05)
7 Bookends (2:35)
8 Fakin' It (1:23)
9 Punky's Dilemma (3:19)
10 Mrs Robinson (2:17)
11 A Hazy Shade Of Winter (2:17)
12 At The Zoo (2:22)

Total album length: 30 minutes

BOOKENDS/SIMON & GARFUNKEL

35 Cheap Thrills

• **Album sales:** 2,000,000 | • **Release date:** September 1968

Cheap Thrills effectively introduced the world to the gifted but tragic singer Janis Joplin. Signed by Columbia Records following its triumphant appearance at 1967's Monterey Pop Festival (and a mid-charting, small-label debut LP), the band had the recording budget and promotional push of the world's largest record company at its back. But it faced the problem encountered by most of the new San Francisco rock groups: how to capture the excitement of their live performances on record. After several unsatisfactory attempts at recording in concert, the band retired to Columbia's studios in New York and Los Angeles and, in 10 days' time, delivered *Cheap Thrills*.

To the musicians and producer John Simon's credit, the album largely succeeds in replicating the group's live sound. Joplin's intense and intimate blues wailing animates 'Piece Of My Heart', a Number Four single on the Hot 100, and her version of Big Mama Thornton's 'Ball and Chain', long a staple of FM-rock radio playlists. The latter, with 'Combination Of The Two', showcases guitarists James Gurley and Sam Andrews' unconventional style, a string-bending, at times dissonant approach that was a key part of Big Brother's signature sound.

Cheap Thrills sold two million copies, but Joplin soon left for a brief but successful solo career, dying of a heroin overdose in 1970.

Number One singles:
None

Grammy awards: None

Label: US: Columbia;
UK: CBS

Recorded in: New York &
Los Angeles, USA

Personnel:
Janis Joplin (d. 1970)
Sam Andrew
James Gurley
David Getz
John Simon
Peter Albin
Roy Segal
John Simon

Producers:
Bob Irwin
John Simon
Elliot Mazer

1 **Combination Of The Two** (5:47)
2 **I Need A Man To Love** (4:54)
3 **Summertime** (4:00)
4 **Piece Of My Heart** (4:15)
5 **Turtle Blues** (4:22)
6 **O Sweet Mary** (4:16)
7 **Ball And Chain** (9:37)

Total album length: 37 minutes

Sleeve artwork by Robert Crumb

34 The Graduate

| • **Album sales:** 2,000,000 | • **Release date:** October 1968 |

For an album that contained only five cuts by the duo, it might seem odd that *The Graduate* became Simon & Garfunkel's first Number One LP (a ranking it maintained for nine consecutive weeks). The soundtrack to Mike Nichols' 1967 film of the same (which introduced Dustin Hoffman), *The Graduate* collected four previously released Simon & Garfunkel songs, including their initial hit, 1966's 'The Sound Of Silence'. The delicate 'April Come She Will' and the harmonically converging 'Scarborough Fair/Canticle' were reprised from the duo's second album, *Parsley, Sage, Rosemary & Thyme*.

The Graduate's most popular and enduring track, though, was its one new Simon & Garfunkel original, commissioned expressly for use in the film. The sly, pop-folk ditty 'Mrs. Robinson' (about Anne Bancroft's older-woman character who seduces Hoffman's Benjamin Braddock) became Simon & Garfunkel's second US Number One single (it reached Number Four in the UK) and remains a concert favourite.

The soundtrack's five other selections are instrumentals from the movie score, performed by arranger Dave Grusin. *The Graduate* became America's top-grossing film of 1968 and was nominated for nine Oscars; Nichols won the Academy Award for Best Director that year.

Number One singles:
US: Mrs Robinson

Grammy Awards:
Record of the Year; Best contemporary pop performance

Label: US: Columbia; UK: CBS

Recorded in: N/A

Personnel:
Art Garfunkel
Paul Simon
Dave Grusin

Producer:
Teo Macero

1 The Sound Of Silence (3:06)
2 The Singleman Party Foxtrot (2:53)
3 On The Strip (2:00)
4 Sunporch Cha-Cha-Cha (2:54)
5 Mrs Robinson (1:15)
6 A Great Effect (4:07)
7 Scarborough Fair/Canticle (6:22)
8 April Come She Will (1:51)
9 Whew (2:12)
10 The Folks (2:28)
11 The Big Bright Green Pleasure Machine (1:46)

Total album length: 31 minutes

Wichita Lineman

| • **Album sales:** 2,000,000 | • **Release date:** November 1968 |

Glen Campbell's only Number One album (it also topped Billboard's country chart), *Wichita Lineman* takes its title from his second Jimmy Webb-penned triumph, a Top Five single on the pop and country charts in 1968.

In terms of both the choice of material and Campbell's performances, *Wichita Lineman* was his strongest collection to date. The title cut is a shimmering gem of a pop song, and the poignant jazz waltz 'Dreams Of The Everyday Housewife', likewise a pop and country hit, is almost as good. Campbell reads Tim Hardin's 'Reason to Believe' with an intimacy that suggests the much-recorded song was written for him. The closing tune, 'That's Not Home', is the album's sleeper, a powerful relationship-ending song that Campbell invests with real pathos. It far outshines 'You Better Sit Down,

Kids', Sonny Bono's take on the same subject, which Campbell handles effectively; the original was a hit for Cher in 1967. Billy Ed Wheeler's 'Ann' is a brisk, lighthearted country tune. *Wichita Lineman*'s complement of contemporary pop tunes includes the Bee Gees' 'Words' and Otis Redding's '(Sittin' on) The Dock of the Bay', which get adequate, if not special, treatment.

Campbell had his own weekly variety show, *The Glen Campbell Goodtime Hour*, which ran from January 1969 until June 1972.

Number One singles: None	**Recorded in:** N/A
	Personnel:
Grammy awards: None	Glen Campbell
Label: US: Capitol; UK: Ember	**Producer:** Al DeLory

1 Wichita Lineman (3:06)
2 (Sittin' On) The Dock Of The Bay (2:32)
3 If You Go Away (3:41)
4 Ann (1:58)
5 Words (2:47)
6 Fate Of Man (2:40)
7 Dreams Of The Everyday Housewife (2:35)
8 Straight Life (2:59)
9 Reason To Believe (2:20)
10 You Better Sit Down, Kids (3:15)
11 That's Not Home (2:45)

Total album length: 31 minutes

Glen Campbell

Glen Campbell
WICHITA LINEMAN

32 Tommy

| • **Album sales:** 2,000,000 | • **Release date:** May 1969 |

Despite having edged onto the Hot 100 as early as 1965, The Who, an established act in their native UK, had never broken big in America. *Tommy* quickly changed that, climbing to Number Five and remaining on Billboard's album chart for more than two years.

Preceded in the 'rock opera' arena by the stage musical *Hair* and *Pretty Things* (both 1968), the Townsend-penned story of a 'deaf, dumb and blind kid' who played a mean pinball worked on a number of levels. First, the score effectively advances the dramatic narrative. Secondly, *Tommy* features some of The Who's sharpest tracks. Among the best are the hit singles, the insistent 'Pinball Wizard' and the liberating, light-headed 'I'm Free'.

Townsend's material has proved resilient. Since this debut, *Tommy* has been staged twice as a musical and once, in 1975, as a successful film, The film version was directed by Ken Russel, starred Daltrey as Tommy and featured a host of famous faces including Oliver Reed, Elton John, Jack Nicholson and Tina Turner.

The album for *Tommy* was recorded at IBC Studio, London and was originally released as a two-LP set with a thin booklet of lyrics and artwork in a triptych-style fold-out cover.

Number One singles:
None

Grammy awards: None

Label: US: Decca;
UK: Track

Recorded in: London, UK

Personnel:
Pete Townsend
John Entwistle (d. 2002)
Keith Moon (d. 1978)
Roger Daltrey

Producers:
Kit Lambert
Chris Stamp

1   Overture (5:21)
2   It's A Boy (0:38)
3   1921 (2:49)
4   Amazing Journey (3:25)
5   Sparks (3:46)
6   Eyesight For The Blind (2:13)
7   Miracle Cure (0:12)
8   Sally Simpson (4:12)
9   I'm Free (2:40)
10 Welcome (4:34)
11 Tommy's Holiday Camp (0:57)
12 We're Not Gonna Take It (7:08)
13 Christmas (4:34)
14 Cousin Kevin (4:07)
15 The Acid Queen (3:34)
16 Underture (10:09)
17 Do You Think It's Alright (0:24)
18 Fiddle About (1:29)
19 Pinball Wizard (3:01)
20 There's A Doctor (0:23)
21 Go To The Mirror (3:49)
22 Tommy Can You Hear Me (1:36)
23 Smash The Mirror (1:35)

Total album length: 73 minutes

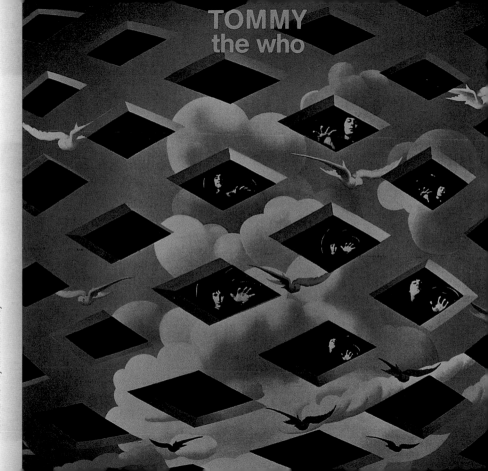

TOMMY
the who

Sleeve artwork by Mike McInnerney

Bayou Country

| • **Album sales:** 2,000,000 | • **Release date:** June 1969 |

Most of the world was first introduced to Creedence Clearwater Revival on this, the band's sophomore album. It was preceded by the group's first million-selling single, 'Proud Mary', featured here among six John Fogerty originals and a cover of another rock classic, Little Richard's 'Good Golly Miss Molly'.

It's important to recall that Creedence did its share of rock-festival performances (including Woodstock, the same year *Bayou Country* was released), and the band were well-used to getting a crowd on its feet. Tunes like the thick-stirred 'Born On The Bayou' and the extended jam 'Keep On Chooglin'' surely filled that role, as did the shorter, riff-reliant 'Bootleg'. 'Penthouse Pauper' is, after 'Proud Mary', the most

distinctive track; Fogerty stretches one of the album's strongest vocals across a taut funk rhythm spiked by tremolo guitar fills.

Bayou Country was one of three Creedence albums released in 1969 and a fitting prelude to the second, *Green River*, on which the band more fully realized its ambitions. The group's trademark song, 'Proud Mary', was an international hit for Ike & Tina Turner (1971) and has been recorded by, among others, Elvis Presley and Solomon Burke.

Number One singles:
None

Grammy awards: None

Label: US: Fantasy;
UK: Liberty

Recorded in: N/A

Personnel:
John Fogerty
Stu Cook
Doug Clifford
Tom Fogerty (d. 1990)

Producer:
John Fogerty

1 **Born On The Bayou** (5:16)
2 **Bootleg** (3:02)
3 **Graveyard Train** (8:37)
4 **Good Golly Miss Molly** (2:44)
5 **Penthouse Pauper** (3:39)
6 **Keep On Chooglin'** (7:41)
7 **Proud Mary** (3:08)

Total album length: 34 minutes

Creedence Clearwater Revival

BAYOU COUNTRY

CREEDENCE CLEARWATER REVIVAL

Sleeve artwork by Basul Parik

30 Santana

| • **Album sales:** 2,000,000 | • **Release date:** August 1969 |

Carlos Santana and his band's debut was among the bigger splashes made by San Francisco's second wave of acid-rock albums. Buoyed by the group's incendiary live shows (Santana played the Woodstock festival in August 1969), *Santana* became a best-selling set, with a 108-week stay on the Billboard chart.

The band shared much with its Bay Area brethren, namely a love of the jam and crowd-pleasing displays of instrumental dexterity. Santana, though, had distinctive stylistic underpinnings in its Latin music influences and deep rhythm section (the album features no less than four percussionists). 'Evil Ways', the group's first Top 10 single, puts both qualities to good use; its Hammond organ groove is irresistible, and Carlos' solo unfurls with a sense of utter freedom. The conga-driven original 'Persuasion' and Nigerian drummer Olatunji's 'Jingo' are almost as impressive, while the show-closing 'Soul Sacrifice' offers the mandatory but not unpleasant long improvisational track.

The band followed *Santana* with the Number One album *Abraxas*. Early Santana members Rollie and Schon left to form Journey in 1973, but Carlos Santana's career has continued to flourish to the present day.

Number One singles:
None

Grammy awards: None

Label: US: Columbia;
UK: CBS

Recorded in: California,
USA

Producer:
Brent Dangerfield

Personnel:
Carlos Santana
Gregg Rolie
David Brown
Neal Schon
Luis Gasca
Jose Chepito Areas
Mike Carabello
Michael Shrieve
Coke Escovedo
Tower of Power

1 Waiting (4:07)
2 Evil Ways (4:00)
3 Shades Of Time (3:14)
4 Savour (2:46)
5 Jin-Go-La-Ba (4:23)
6 Persuasion (2:37)
7 Treat (4:46)
8 You Just Don't Care (4:37)
9 Soul Sacrifice (6:38)

Total album length: 37 minutes

Santana

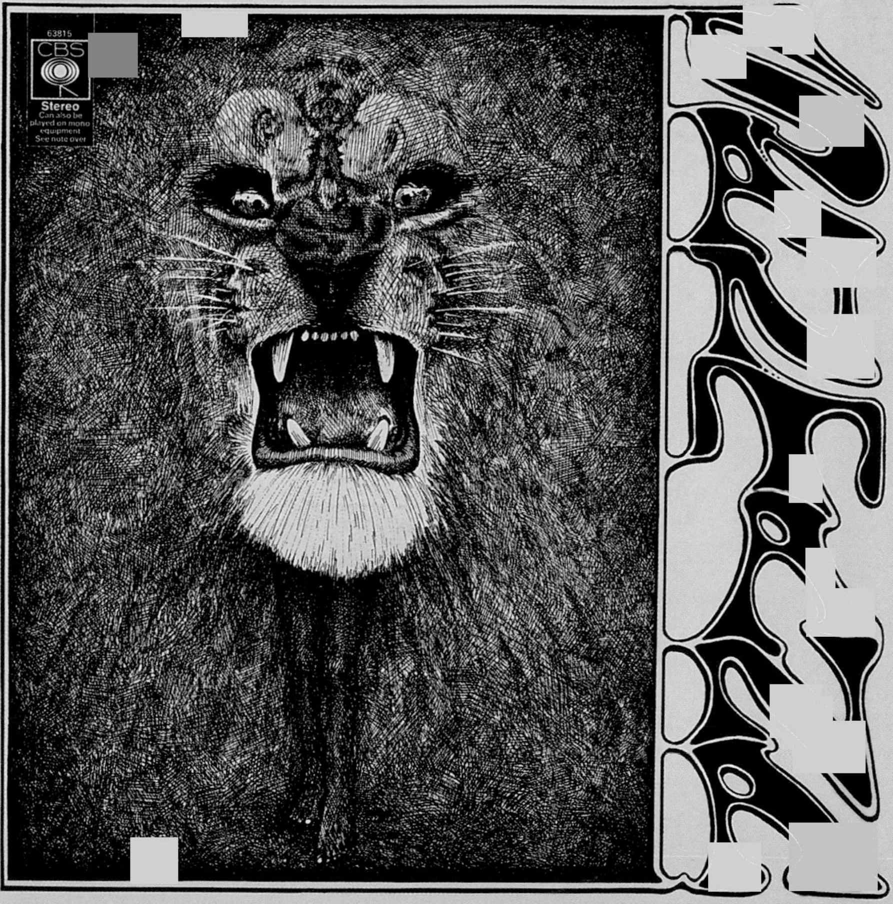

Sleeve artwork by Lee Conklin

The Chicago Transit Authority

| • **Album sales:** 2,000,000 | • **Release date:** December 1969 |

Two of the more eventful developments in late-1960s rock were the advent of heavy metal and the formation of bands with full horn sections. The former trend proved deathless, the latter more short-lived, with the notable exception of Chicago.

By the time of their double-album debut, the Windy City seven-piece shared the brass-rock crown with just one other band, Blood, Sweat & Tears. *The Chicago Transit Authority* connected with both the AM radio audience ('Does Anybody Really Know What Time It Is?' and 'Beginnings' were both Top 10 singles) and the FM-rock crowd (with the band's cover of the Spencer Davis Group's 'I'm a Man').

Chicago's combination of trumpet, trombone and reeds with the conventional guitars-drums-keyboard set-up made for powerful, punchy music, and it could swing, as on 'Does Anybody Really Know What Time It Is?' It helped that beneath the brass were solidly built tunes and that the band's vocalists had a knack for harmonies (the group recorded later with The Beach Boys) as well as husky leads. In time, these vocal-group abilities would serve Chicago particularly well, as romantic ballads became a mainstay of its repertoire.

The Chicago Transit Authority stayed on Billboard's album chart for more than three years.

Number One singles:
None

Grammy awards: None

Label: US: Columbia;
UK: CBS

Recorded in:
Los Angeles, USA

Personnel:
Robert Lamm
Terry Kath (d. 1978)
Peter Cetera
Dan Seraphine
Lee Loughnane
James Pankow
Walter Parazaider

Producer:
James William Guercio

1   Introduction (6:35)
2   Does Anybody Really Know What Time It Is? (4:36)
3   Beginnings (7:54)
4   Questions 67 And 68 (5:02)
5   Listen (3:21)
6   Poems 58 (8:37)
7   Free From Guitar (6:47)
8   South California Purples (6:11)
9   I'm A Man (7:39)
10 Prologue August 29, 1968 (0:57)
11 Someday (4:13)
12 Liberation (14:38)

Total album length: 79 minutes

Chicago

Sleeve artwork by Nick Fasciano

Willie And The Poor Boys

| **Album sales:** 2,000,000 | **Release date:** October 1969 |

Blistering rock 'n' roll and uncompromising social comment characterize the fourth Creedence Clearwater Revival album. *Willie And The Poor Boys* was released barely three months after *Green River*, to a record-buying public that could not get enough of California's fierce little 'travelin' band'. The album reached the Top 10 on both the US and UK album charts.

Willie still has room for the band's familiar swamp-rock ('Feelin' Blue' could be a *Green River* outtake) and even good-time pop ('Down On The Corner'), but much of its material is of a more serious cast. 'Don't Look Now (It Ain't You Or Me)' seems to criticize the youth culture of the time, which preached equality but often practiced privilege. More pointed still is

'Fortunate Son'. The hard-driving other half of the hit single 'Down on the Corner' takes square aim at the hypocrisy of the Vietnam war, specifically the senators' and millionaires' high-born offspring who avoided the draft.

The other hard rocker is 'It Came Out Of The Sky', an affectionately torrid tribute to such 1950s alien-invasion sagas as 'Flying Saucers Rock and Roll'. Roots respect is also extended to traditional folk blues via covers of 'The Midnight Special' and Leadbelly's 'Cotton Fields'.

Number One singles:
None

Grammy awards: None

Label: US: Fantasy;
UK: Liberty

Recorded in: N/A

Personnel:
John Fogerty
Stu Cook
Doug Clifford
Tom Fogerty (d. 1990)

Producer:
John Fogerty

1 **Down On The Corner** (2:47)
2 **It Came Out Of The Sky** (2:56)
3 **Cotton Fields** (2:54)
4 **Poor Boy Shuffle** (2:27)
5 **Feelin' Blue** (5:05)
6 **Fortunate Son** (2:21)
7 **Don't Look Now** (2:12)
8 **The Midnight Special** (4:14)
9 **Side Of The Road** (3:26)
10 **Effigy** (6:31)

Total album length: 35 minutes

CREEDENCE CLEARWATER REVIVAL

DUCK KEE MARKET

EER · WINE · FROZEN FOOD · PRODUCE · MEAT

TON'S

WILLY AND THE POOR BOYS

27 Let It Bleed

| • **Album sales:** 2,000,000 | • **Release date:** November 1969 |

*L*et It Bleed was released at the end of one of the most tumultuous years of The Rolling Stones' career. Founding member Brian Jones quit the band, then died unexpectedly of a drug overdose. A murder occurred in the audience during the group's Altamont rock-festival performance. The murder, coming so soon after the death of Jones, had a harrowing effect on Keith Richards and his reaction was to increase his use of heroin.

Released in the fall of 1969, *Let It Bleed* was comprised of sessions with Jones and Taylor, yet it continued the direction of *Beggars Banquet*, signalling that a new era in the Stones' career had begun, one marked by ragged music and an increasingly wasted sensibility.

The album nonetheless stands as one of their finest, for the strength of its material and the energized performances of the band and its sizable supporting cast. Not only is Jones' replacement, guitarist Mick Taylor, aboard, but so are keyboard players Al Kooper and Nicky Hopkins, horn men and a choir (which handles the *a cappella* intro to the classic 'You Can't Always Get What You Want').

Number One singles:
None

Grammy awards: None

Label: US: London;
UK: Decca

Recorded in: London, UK
and Los Angeles, USA

Personnel:
Mick Jagger
Keith Richards
Bill Wyman

Mick Taylor
Brian Jones (d. 1969)
Al Kooper
Jack Nitzsche
Ry Cooder
Nicky Hopkins
Charlie Watts
Ian Stewart
Doris Troy
Nanette Newman
Various other personnel

Producer:
Jimmy Miller

1 **Gimmie Shelter** (4:30)
2 **Love In Vain** (4:19)
3 **Country Honk** (3:07)
4 **Live With Me** (3:33)
5 **Let It Bleed** (5:27)
6 **Midnight Rambler** (6:52)
7 **You Got The Silver** (2:50)
8 **Monkey Man** (4:11)
9 **You Can't Always Get What You Want** (7:28)

Total album length: 43 minutes

Blue Hawaii

| • **Album sales:** 3,000,000 | • **Release date:** December 1961 |

Presley's fourth soundtrack collection *Blue Hawaii*, from the 1961 motion picture, yielded the singer's seventh Number One album. It ruled the Billboard chart for 20 weeks in a row and the UK charts for 18 weeks. *Blue Hawaii* featured one of Presley's most convincing early ballads, RCA producer-writers Hugo Peretti and Luigi Creatore's 'Can't Help Falling In Love', which made Number One in the UK and Number Two in the US. The single's nonsense-rock flipside, 'Rock-A-Hula, Baby', was a Top 30 hit.

Among the 'traditional' Hawaiian songs are the title track (originally written for Bing Crosby in the 1930s) and 'Hawaiian Wedding Song' (the island standard was a pop hit for Andy Williams in 1959). Though the album has more than its share of lightweight material ('Slicin' Sand', 'Ito Eats'), Presley seems to take some genuine delight in the bluesy 'Beach Boy Blues', in which he is backed by the Jordanaires.

So successful was the *Blue Hawaii* movie, grossing over $31 million (£16.75 million) at the box office, that a second Presley island epic, *Paradise, Hawaiian Style*, was commissioned and released in 1966.

Number One singles:
UK: Can't Help Falling In Love

Grammy awards:
None

Label: UK & US: RCA

Recorded in: London, UK & New York, USA

Personnel:
Elvis Presley (d. 1977)
The Jordanaires
The Surfers
Scotty Moore
Hank Garland
Tiny Timbrell
Alvino Rey
Various musicians

Producer:
Don Wardell

1 Blue Hawaii (2.35)
2 Almost Always True (2.24)
3 Aloha Oe (1.54)
4 No More (2.22)
5 Can't Help Falling In Love (2.59)
6 Rock-A-Hula, Baby (1.58)
7 Moonlight Swim (2.18)
8 Ku-U-I-Po (2.20)
9 Ito Eats (1.25)
10 Slicin' Sand (1.34)
11 Hawaiian Sunset (2.30)
12 Beach Boy Blues (2.00)
13 Island of Love (2.40)
14 Hawaiian Wedding Song (2.48)

Total album length: 32 minutes

Elvis Presley

RCA

VICTOR

PRESENTS
AN ORIGINAL SOUND TRACK ALBUM
14 GREAT SONGS

SEE
ELVIS
IN HAL WALLIS'

BLUE
HAWAII

14 GREAT
SONGS

AN ORIGINAL
SOUNDTRACK
RECORDING

25 West Side Story

| • **Album sales:** 3,000,000 | • **Release date:** December 1961 |

Leonard Bernstein and Stephen Sondheim's music for *West Side Story* is one of the most acclaimed works in American theatre and popular music. This soundtrack album to the film adaptation of the 1957 musical topped Billboard's chart for 54 weeks.

The score contributed a half dozen uncontested standards to the pop repertoire. The best known is probably 'Somewhere', which has been recorded by countless artists (Barbra Streisand and pop rocker Len Barry charted with singles of it). The romantic ballad 'Tonight' has likewise enjoyed hundreds of cover versions, including a Top 10 hit for pianists Ferrante & Teicher (1961), and there's hardly a cabaret act that doesn't include one of the above or the

anxious 'Something's Coming' in its stage repertoire. The tunes are sung here by Marni Nixon and Jim Bryant, for Natalie Wood's Maria character and Richard Beymer's Tony.

The operatic 'Maria' (Bryant) has seen its share of recordings, as well, and the juvenile-delinquent rap 'Cool' (Tucker Smith and the Jets) was an early influence on rocker Alice Cooper, who titled his second album *Easy Action* after a line in the song.

Number One singles:
None

Grammy awards: None

Label: US & UK: CBS

Recorded in: California, USA

Personnel:
Natalie Wood
Richard Beymer
Russ Tamblyn
Rita Moreno
George Chakiris
Various Artists

Producers:
Didier C. Deusch

1 Prologue (6:37)
2 Jet Song (2:06)
3 Something's Coming (2:32)
4 Dance At The Gym (9:24)
5 Maria (2:34)
6 America (4:59)
7 Tonight (5:43)
8 Gee, Officer Krupke (4:14)
9 I Feel Pretty (3:35)
10 One Hand, One Heart (3:02)
11 Quintet (3:22)
12 The Rumble (2:39)
13 Cool (4:21)
14 A Boy Like That/I Have A Love (4:28)
15 Somewhere (finale) (4:20)

Total album length: 64 minutes

THE ORIGINAL SOUND TRACK RECORDING

"WEST SIDE STORY"

ROBERT WISE
PRESENTS

NATALIE WOOD

RICHARD BEYMER
RUSS TAMBLYN
RITA MORENO
GEORGE CHAKIRIS

ROBERT WISE and JEROME ROBBINS

ERNEST LEHMAN

JEROME ROBBINS

LEONARD BERNSTEIN

STEPHEN SONDHEIM

ARTHUR LAURENTS

JEROME ROBBINS

CONDUCTED BY JOHNNY GREEN

WEST
SIDE
STORY

24 Help!

• **Album sales:** 3,000,000 │ • **Release date:** July 1965

*H*elp! was the soundtrack to the Beatles' second movie and was the band's sixth Number One album in the US, a position it held for nine weeks. In the UK, a vastly different configuration of the record substituted additional Beatles tracks for Ken Thorne's movie-score selections and also topped the chart.

The US version of *Help!* contains only the seven Beatles tracks that actually appear in the film, but they're all first-rate. Among them are two Number One hits, the somewhat folk-rockish title cut and the highly imaginative 'Ticket to Ride'. More conventional Lennon–McCartney fare includes 'The Night Before', 'Another Girl', and Lennon's faux-Dylan 'You've Go To Hide Your Love Away'. George Harrison's contribution, 'I Need You', provides a refreshing change of pace.

Help! premiered in New York in August 1965, just as The Beatles commenced their third US tour. The same month, the soundtrack album wrested the UK's top slot from 'Mr. Tambourine Man', the debut by the Beatles-inspired Byrds.

Number One singles: US & UK: Help!; Ticket To Ride

Grammy awards: None

Label: US: Capitol; UK: Parlophone

Recorded in: London, UK

Producers:
George Martin
Dave Dexter, Jr

Personnel:
John Lennon (d. 1980)
Paul McCartney
George Harrison (d. 2001)
Ringo Starr
George Martin
Kenneth Essex
Francisco Gabarro
Tony Gilbert
Sidney Sax
John Scott

US:
1 Help! (2:35)
2 The Night Before (2:33)
3 From Me to You Fantasy (Instrumental) (2:03)
4 You've Got to Hide Your Love Away (2:08)
5 I Need You (2:28)
6 In the Tyrol (Instrumental) (2:21)
7 Another Girl (2:02)
8 Another Hard Day's Night (Instrumental) (2:28)
9 Ticket to Ride (3:03)
10 Bitter End (2:20)
11 You're Gonna Lose That Girl (2:18)
12 Chase (Instrumental) (2:24)

Total album length: 29 minutes

UK:
1 Help! (2:30)
2 The Night Before (2:37)
3 You've Got To Hide Your Love Away (2:11)
4 I Need You (2:32)
5 Another Girl (2:08)
6 You're Gonna To Lose That Girl (2:20)
7 Ticket To Ride (3:13)
8 Act Naturally (2:33)
9 It's Only Love (1:59)
10 You Like Me Too Much (2:38)
11 Tell Me What You See (2:40)
12 I've Just Seen Your Face (2:07)
13 Yesterday (2:08)
14 Dizzy Miss Lizzy (5:54)

Total album length: 38 minutes

THE BEATLES

HELP!

Sleeve artwork by Robert Freeman

23 Beatles '65

| • **Album sales:** 3,000,000 | • **Release date:** January 1965 |

The Beatles' fourth Number One album, *Beatles '65* was a US-only LP, though it drew many of its tracks from the UK collection *Beatles For Sale*. *Beatles '65* topped the Billboard album chart for nine weeks.

If there's a common theme to the material on *Beatles '65*, it's the record's lighter, almost folkish tone, not surprising considering the album's namesake year. This flavour is most noticeable in the largely acoustic arrangement of the 'I'll Be Back,' 'I'll Follow The Sun' and the affectingly laid-back 'No Reply'. 'I'm a Loser', with its jangling rhythm and Lennon's Dylan-ish harmonica solo, is pure folk-rock.

It's a pair of harder rockers, though, that gave the album its only significant singles action. The double-sided 'I Feel Fine'/ 'She's a Woman' hit chart peaks of Number One and Number Four, respectively. This portion of the program is rounded out by an appropriately raucous version of Chuck Berry's 'Rock and Roll Music'.

The most adventurous track is 'Baby's In Black' an almost Buck Owens-ish country waltz with a gorgeous bridge and a Lennon lead vocal. Among a handful of covers, 'Honey Don't' (with Ringo on lead) and 'Everybody's Trying To Be My Baby' come from the repertoire of Harrison's idol, Sun Records rockabilly star Carl Perkins.

Number One singles: US & UK: I Feel Fine

Grammy awards: None

Label: US: Capitol; UK: Parlophone

Recorded in: N/A

Personnel:
John Lennon (d. 1980)
Paul McCartney
George Harrison (d. 2001)
Ringo Starr
George Martin

Producer:
George Martin

1 No Reply (2:18)
2 I'm A Loser (2:33)
3 Baby's In Black (2:08)
4 Rock And Roll Music (2:34)
5 I'll Follow The Sun (1:51)
6 Mr Moonlight (2:37)
7 Honey Don't (3:00)
8 I'll Be Back (2:21)
9 She's A Woman (3:03)
10 I Feel Fine (2:20)
11 Everybody's Trying To Be My Baby (2:24)

Total album length: 27 minutes

The Beatles

GREAT NEW HITS BY JOHN • PAUL • GEORGE • RINGO

BEATLES '65

HIGH FIDELITY

I FEEL FINE • SHE'S A WOMAN • NO REPLY • I'M A LOSER • ROCK AND ROLL MUSIC • I'LL FOLLOW THE SUN •
HONEY DON'T • I'LL BE BACK • BABY'S IN BLACK • EVERYBODY'S TRYING TO BE MY BABY • MR. MOONLIGHT

22 Sounds Of Silence

| • **Album sales:** 3,000,000 | • **Release date:** March 1966 |

Simon & Garfunkel's 'The Sound of Silence' and the Byrds' 'Mr. Tambourine Man' were the twin defining moments of folk-rock, even if the former enjoyed a less than organic origin.

While Paul Simon visited England in 1965, in New York the duo's producer added amplified backing to the acoustic track, which had been issued on their previous album. Released as a single, the electrified version topped the Hot 100 for two weeks, obliging Simon & Garfunkel to quickly assemble an album to accompany it. The title song was released previously on the album *Wednesday Morning, 3 A.M.*, and also on the soundtrack to the movie *The Graduate*.

Consisting almost entirely of Simon originals,

Sounds Of Silence introduced the pop public to the songwriter's considerable talent. The outline of his maturing style is first sketched in the narrative vignettes 'A Most Peculiar Man' and 'Somewhere They Can't Find Me', the imagistic 'Leaves That Are Green' and the more directly personal 'I Am A Rock'. Of the two non-originals, 'Richard Cory' is an adaptation of an Edward Arlington Robinson poem and the instrumental 'Angie' a cover of a tune by British guitarist Davey Graham.

'I Am A Rock' was Simon & Garfunkel's third Top Five hit, released as a single following their second, 'Homeward Bound', from 1966's *Parsley, Sage, Rosemary and Thyme*. That set, like *Sounds Of Silence*, was produced by Bob Johnston.

Number One singles:
US: The Sound Of Silence
(UK: unreleased)

Grammy Awards: None

Label: US: Columbia;
UK: CBS

Recorded in: Nashville
and Los Angeles, USA

Personnel:
Art Garfunkel
Paul Simon

Producer:
Bob Johnston

1 **The Sound Of Silence** (3:03)
2 **Leaves That Are Green** (2:20)
3 **Blessed** (3:13)
4 **Kathy's Song** (3:17)
5 **Somewhere They Can't Find Me** (2:34)
6 **Angie** (2:13)
7 **Homeward Bound** (2:30)

8 **Richard Cory** (2:54)
9 **A Most Peculiar Man** (2:29)
10 **April Come She Will** (1:48)
11 **We've Got A Groove Thing Goin'** (1:56)
12 **I Am A Rock** (2:49)

Total album length: 26 minutes

CBS

32020

SIMON & GARFUNKEL
SOUNDS OF SILENCE
including 'Homeward Bound'

Parsley, Sage, Rosemary and Thyme

| • **Album sales:** 3,000,000 | • **Release date:** October 1966 |

Surely 1966 ranks as one of the most creative years in pop history. Poised between the immediate post-Beatles rush and the dawn of psychedelia, it is marked by the fresh sound of artists finding their own voices – on adventurous and commercially successful albums like *Aftermath*, *Blonde on Blonde* and *Revolver*.

Parsley, Sage, Rosemary and Thyme is, in many ways, the first real Simon & Garfunkel album. Present for the first time are the layered 'choir-boy' vocal arrangements that would become the duo's trademark. Poetic, rhythmic and resolutely tuneful, the songs were also extremely short with much of the material barely surpassing the two-minute mark, culminating in 12 songs that don't add up to half an hour.

Political as well as personal concerns occupy the album. '7 O'Clock News/Silent Night' intercuts the Christmas hymn with TV reports of Vietnam war casualties and the Dylan parody 'A Simple Desultory Philippic' takes shots at US government policy and pop culture.

'Homeward Bound' about life on the road while Simon was touring in England in 1965 reached Number Five on the Hot 100, and 'The Dangling Conversation' made the Top 30. The much-covered 'Feelin' Groovy' was a hit single for Harper's Bizarre in 1967.

Number One singles:
None

Grammy awards: None

Label: US: Columbia;
UK: CBS

Recorded in: N/A

Personnel:
Art Garfunkel
Paul Simon

Producer:
Bob Johnston

1 Scarborough Fair/Canticle (3:08)
2 Patterns (2:42)
3 Cloudy (2:10)
4 Homeward Bound (2:30)
5 The Big Bright Green Pleasure Machine (2:42)
6 The 59th Street Bridge Song (Feelin' Groovy) (1:43)
7 The Dangling Conversation (2:37)
8 Flowers Never Bend With The Rainfall (2:10)
9 A Simple Desultory Philippic (Or How I Was Robert McNamara'd Into Submission) (2:12)
10 For Emily, Whenever I May Find Her (2:04)
11 A Poem On The Underground (1:52)
12 7 O'Clock News/Silent Night (2:01)

Total album length: 28 minutes

Simon and Garfunkel

Parsley, Sage, Rosemary and Thyme

Homeward Bound
The Dangling Conversation
Scarborough Fair / Canticle
Patterns
For Emily, Whenever I May Find Her
The Big Bright Green Pleasure Machine
A Poem on the Underground Wall
Cloudy
A Simple Desultory Philippic (Or How I Was
Robert McNamara'd Into Submission)
The 59th St. Bridge Song (Feelin' Groovy)
Flowers Never Bend With the Rainfall
7 O'Clock News / Silent Night

At Folsom Prison

| • **Album sales:** 3,000,000 | • **Release date:** January 1968 |

Johnny Cash

This recording of a concert at a California penitentiary in front of 2,000 convicted felons initiated Cash's ascent to icon status. Cash had already been a rockabilly star, notched country hits and occasionally crossed over into Top 40 territory. But something about *At Folsom Prison* – the song selection, energized performances and spirited audience reaction – resonated universally with the public. The album sold more than three million copies.

Folsom's repertoire is rich in the themes and attitudes audiences have long loved in Cash's music. The title track is joined in its joyous defiance by 'Cocaine Blues' and the condemned-man saga '25 Minutes To Go'.

At Folsom Prison made Cash fans of country enthusiasts, folk purists, college students and conservatives, staying on Billboard's album chart more than two years. The title-track single gave Cash a Top 40 pop hit and his eighth Number One country hit.

Number One singles:
None

Grammy awards:
Best album notes; Best male country vocal performance; Best country & western performance duet, trio or group

Label:
US: Columbia; UK: CBS

Recorded in: California, USA

Personnel:
Johnny Cash (d. 2003)
Al Casey
June Carter Cash (d. 2003)
Luther Perkins
Marshall Grant
W. S. Holland
The Carter Family
The Statler Brothers

Producers:
Bob Johnston

1   **Folsom Prison Blues** (2:42)
2   **Dark As A Dungeon** (3:04)
3   **I Still Miss Someone** (1:37)
4   **Cocaine Blues** (3:01)
5   **25 Minutes To Go** (3:31)
6   **Orange Blossom Special** (3:00)
7   **The Long Black Veil** (3:57)
8   **Send A Picture Of Mother** (2:10)
9   **The Wall** (1:36)
10 **Dirty Old Egg Sucking Dog** (1:30)
11 **Flushed From The Bathroom Of Your Heart** (2:17)
12 **Jackson** (3:12)
13 **Give My Love To Rose** (2:40)
14 **I Got Stripes** (1:57)
14 **Green Green Grass Of Home** (2:29)
14 **Greystone Chapel** (6:02)

Total album length: 45 minutes

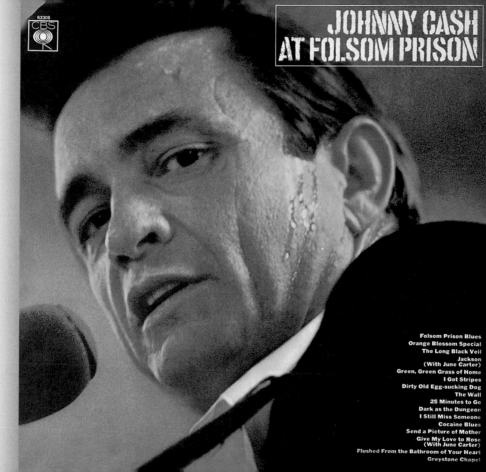

CBS

63308

JOHNNY CASH
AT FOLSOM PRISON

Folsom Prison Blues
Orange Blossom Special
The Long Black Veil
Jackson
(With June Carter)
Green, Green Grass of Home
I Got Stripes
Dirty Old Egg-sucking Dog
The Wall
25 Minutes to Go
Dark as the Dungeon
I Still Miss Someone
Cocaine Blues
Send a Picture of Mother
Give My Love to Rose
(With June Carter)
Flushed From the Bathroom of Your Heart
Greystone Chapel

Johnny Cash At San Quentin

| • **Album sales:** 3,000,000 | • **Release date:** August 1969 |

As popular as Cash's *At Folsom Prison* was, its sequel received an even more enthusiastic response from the public. *Johnny Cash At San Quentin*, recorded at California's maximum-security prison, provided the country-music legend with his only Number One album and his biggest single hit, 'A Boy Named Sue'. that went to Number One on the country charts and Number Three on the US pop charts.

Cash's delicious reading of the Shel Silverstein novelty tune resides in good company. The program is well-stocked with reprises of several Cash classics, including 'I Still Miss Someone' and the Sun Records hits 'Big River' and 'I Walk the Line'. As he did on *At Folsom Prison*, Cash is careful to balance the program between rousing crowd-pleasers and inspirational pieces. His original composition 'San Quentin' draws cheers for its unrepentant view of the venue ('San Quentin, may you rot and burn in hell'), and the gospel standard '(There'll Be) Peace in the Valley', performed with Carl Perkins and the Carter Family, draws respectful applause.

The album won Cash a Grammy in the Best male vocal country performance category. Johnny Cash died in 2003.

Number One singles:
None

Grammy awards:
Best male vocal country performance

Label: US: Columbia; UK: CBS

Recorded in: California, USA

Personnel:
Johnny Cash (d. 2003)
Al Casey
June Carter Cash (d. 2003)
The Carter Family

Producer:
Bob Johnston

1   Wanted Man (3:24)
2   Wreck Of The Old 97 (2:04)
3   I Walk The Line (3:29)
4   Darling Companion (3:21)
5   A Boy Named Sue (3:58)
6   Starkville City Jail (6:14)
7   San Quentin (3:24)
8   Peace In The Valley (2:30)
9   Folsome Prison Blues (4:23)

Total album length: 32 minutes

JOHNNY CASH AT SAN QUENTIN

A Boy Named Sue
Wanted Man
I Walk the Line
Wreck of the Old 97
San Quentin
Darling Companion
Starkville City Jail
Folsom Prison Blues

Sleeve artwork by Henry Fox

18

Green River

| • **Album sales:** 3,000,000 | • **Release date:** December 1969 |

By the time Creedence Clearwater Revival released *Green River*, their third album (and first Number One), critics had a name for John Fogerty and bandmates' bottom-heavy roots music: 'swamp rock'.

Green River is where Creedence hit its stride. The album contains three of the group's best-known compositions, in the plaintive bar-band favorite 'Lodi', the ominous country-blues 'Bad Moon Rising' and the irresistible title track. All three were radio hits and concert favourites, with 'Green River' reaching Number Two on the Hot 100 (behind the Archies' 'Sugar Sugar'). Another single, 'Commotion' hints at the political dissatisfaction that surfaces in Creedence songs like 'Fortunate Son' and 'Who'll Stop the Rain'.

The enormous popularity of Creedence's swamp rock bears powerful testimony to the virtues of song craftsmanship and unaffected performance. The hit streak represented by *Green River*, *Willie and the Poor Boys* and their various hits occurred at the same time that some of late-1960s rock's worst excess ran unchecked. Against the endless guitar solos and overwrought vocals of the day, the economy and directness of 'Lodi' and 'Bad Moon Rising' retain dignity as well as enormous drive. The single 'Bad Moon Rising' reached Number One in the US and Number Two in the UK.

Number One singles:
US: Bad Moon Rising

Grammy awards: None

Label: US: Fantasy;
UK: Liberty

Recorded in: N/A

Personnel:
John Fogerty
Stu Cook
Doug Clifford
Tom Fogerty (d. 1990)

Producer:
Saul Zeantz

1 Green River (2:36)
2 Commotion (2:44)
3 Tombstone Shadow (3:39)
4 Wrote A Song For Everyone (4:57)
5 Bad Moon Rising (2:21)
6 Lodi (3:13)
7 Cross-Tie Walker (3:20)
8 Sinister Purpose (3:22)
9 Night Time Is The Right Time (3:08)

Total album length: 29 minutes

GREEN RIVER

CREEDENCE
CLEARWATER
REVIVAL

Sleeve artwork by Basul Parik

Fantasy

Moondance

| • **Album sales:** 3,000,000 | • **Release date:** December 1969 |

Though preceded by 1967's bomb *Blowin' Your Mind* and 1968's critically esteemed *Astral Weeks*, *Moondance* was George Ivan Morrison's (popularly known as Van Morrison) first commercially successful album. As focused and accessible as *Astral Weeks* was expansive and demanding, *Moondance* is one of the 1960s rock's seminal sets.

On it, Morrison lays out the style that has served him ever since: bluesy melodies, punchy reed and brass accents and intensely personal visions delivered in a compelling, soulful manner. The lilting, jazz-like title cut remains his signature song, recorded by dozens of artists over four decades, though 'Crazy Love' has also enjoyed its share of cover versions. The use of vocal support from church-trained female singers, on 'Brand New Day' and 'Crazy Love', reflects the pop-gospel arranging style popular with many rock artists of the early 1970s period.

Of the uptempo tracks, the brisk 'I'll Come Running' was issued as a single peaking at Number 39. *Moondance* peaked at Number 29 on Billboard's Pop Albums chart. Nonetheless, the lasting impact made by *Moondance* was more aesthetic than commercial.

Number One singles: None

Grammy awards: None

Label: US & UK: Warners

Recorded in: London

Personnel:
Van Morrison
Cissy Houston
Collin Tilton
David Shaw
Emily Houston
Gary Mallaber
Guy Masson
Jack Schroer
Jackie Verdell
Jeff Labes
John Klingberg
John Platania
Judy Clay

Producer:
Van Morrison

1   **And It Stoned Me** (4:30)
2   **Moondance** (4:35)
3   **Crazy Love** (2:34)
4   **Into The Mystic** (3:25)
5   **Caravan** (4:57)
6   **Come Running** (2:30)
7   **These Dreams Of You** (3:50)
8   **Brand New Day** (5:09)
9   **Everyone** (3:31)
10 **Glad Tidings** (3:13)

Total album length: 38 minutes

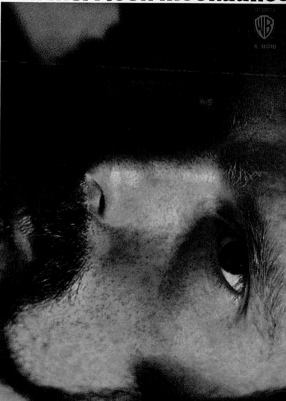

van morrison moondance

STEREO

K 46040

16 A Hard Day's Night

| • **Album sales:** 4,000,000 | • **Release date:** July 1964 |

Though The Beatles are present on only about two thirds of its tracks, the soundtrack to the band's first motion picture – a fictionalized day in the life of the band – gave them their second US Number One album and topped the charts in the UK. The film received two Academy Award nominations, for Best Original Screenplay and Best Adapted Musical Score.

While the British edition of *A Hard Day's Night* was comprised exclusively of 13 Beatles tracks, the US version consisted of George Martin's four instrumental selections from the film, including 1964s mid-charting single 'This Boy (Ringo's Theme)', and the Beatles' cuts. Some of the group's finest pop rock 'n' roll is on display here. The invigorating 'Tell Me Why,' the title track, and 'Can't Buy Me Love' arrange joyous marriages of power and melody. The latter two tracks were US and UK Number One singles.

The Beatles' February 1964 performance on *The Ed Sullivan Show* remains one of the highest rated television programs of all time, with around 73 million people tuning in.

Number One singles:
US & UK: A Hard Day's Night; Can't Buy Me Love

Grammy Awards:
Best performance by a vocal group

Label: US: Capitol; UK: Parlophone

Recorded in: London, UK & Paris, France

Personnel:
John Lennon (d. 1980)
Paul McCartney
George Harrison (d. 2001)
Ringo Starr

Producer:
George Martin

US:
1 A Hard Day's Night (2:28)
2 Tell Me Why (2:04)
3 I'll Cry Instead (2:06)
4 I Should Have Known Better (Instrumental) (2:16)
5 I'm Happy Just to Dance With You (1:59)
6 And I Love Her (Instrumental) (3:42)
7 I Should Have Known Better (2:42)
8 If I Fell (2:16)
9 And I Love Her (2:27)
10 This Boy (Instrumental) (3:06)
11 Can't Buy Me Love (2:15)
12 A Hard Day's Night (Instrumental) (2:00)

Total album length: 29 minutes

UK:
1 A Hard Day's Night (2:32)
2 I Should Have Known Better (2:44)
3 If I Fell (2:22)
4 I'm Happy Just To Dance With You (1:58)
5 And I Love Her (2:31)
6 Tell Me Why (2:10)
7 Can't Buy Me Love (2:14)
8 Anytime At All (2:13)
9 I'll Cry Instead (1:47)
10 Things We Said Today (2:38)
11 When I Get Home (2:18)
12 You Can't Do That (2:37)
13 I'll Be Back (2:20)

Total album length: 30 minutes

THE BEATLES

PARLOPHONE

Are You Experienced?

| • **Album sales:** 4,000,000 | • **Release date:** May 1967 |

In a pop-music year rich in debuts and breakthrough recordings, Hendrix's arrival stood out. By the time *Are You Experienced?* was released in the US, the expatriate singer-guitarist had notched three Top 10 singles in the UK ('Hey Joe', 'Purple Haze' and 'The Wind Cries Mary') and stolen the show at California's Monterey Pop Festival. However, this hit-single success was not duplicated in the US. With little Top 40 airplay, Hendrix and company promoted their debut with a national tour, and with the enthusiastic aid of the newly emerging 'underground' FM rock stations, many of which began playing the import version of *Are You Experienced?*

Simply put, the album introduces one of rock music's seminal artists. Blues is the basis for such songs as 'Foxy Lady' and 'Fire', but Hendrix's compositions and performances stretch the root form into something utterly original and unprecedented.

Hendrix revolutionized the way amplified guitar was played, and not just with his way with bruising blues licks. Tracks such as 'May This Be Love' and the stunning 'Wind Cries Mary' display as much beauty and sensitivity as the rockers exhibit raw power. Hendrix likewise proves himself an impressive vocalist, as he animates the album's songs of love, lust, interstellar travel and drug disorientation.

Number One singles:
None

Grammy Awards: None

Label: US: Reprise;
UK: Track

Recorded in: London, UK

Personnel:
Jimi Hendrix (d. 1970)
Noel Redding (d. 2003)
Mitch Mitchell

Producer:
Chas Chandler

1 Foxy Lady (3:19)
2 Manic Depression (3:42)
3 Red House (3:44)
4 Can You See Me (2:33)
5 Love Or Confusion (3:12)
6 I Don't Live Today (3:55)
7 May This Be Love (3:11)
8 Fire (2:45)
9 Third Stone From The Sun (6:44)
10 Remember (2:48)
11 Are You Experienced? (4:14)

Total album length: 40 minutes

14 In-A-Gadda-Da-Vida

| • **Album sales:** 4,000,000 | • **Release date:** July 1968 |

British outfits like Deep Purple and Black Sabbath are generally credited with inventing heavy metal, but California psychedelic rockers like Blue Cheer ('Summertime Blues') and Iron Butterfly can stake an equally valid claim.

Relentless, minor-key bass riffs, gnarled guitar and funereal organ are the essence of the 17-minute 'In-A-Gadda-Da-Vida', the centerpiece of San Diego-based Iron Butterfly's second album, recorded at Goldstar Studios in Hollywood. The tune began life as a ballroom crowd-pleaser, became an FM-rock favourite and was edited down to a three-minute single, where it helped push its parent album to a 140-week stay on the Billboard chart, 81 weeks on the Top Ten.

The remainder of *In-A-Gadda-Da-Vida* is comprised of five shorter, more pop-ish group originals. A soul riff and a solo inspired by The Doors' 'Light My Fire' somewhat distinguishes 'Most Anything You Want', while 'Flowers and Beads' employs airy harmonies to give off a slight Rascals flavour. Iron Butterfly were awarded the recording industry's first platinum album.

Iron Butterfly continued to chart albums through 1975. The band's metal/stoner-rock credentials are underscored by the fact that *In-A-Gadda-Da-Vida* was Atlantic Records' best-seller until the 1969 arrival of Led Zeppelin – and by a certain resemblance in the two bands' names.

Number One singles:
None

Grammy Awards: None

Label: US: Atco;
UK: Atlantic

Recorded in: Hollywood, USA

Personnel:
Doug Ingle
Erik Braun
Lee Dorman
Ron Bushy

Producer:
Richard Pododor

1 **Most Anything You Want** (3:44)
2 **Flowers And Beads** (3:09)
3 **My Mirage** (4:55)
4 **Termination** (2:53)
5 **Are You Happy** (4:29)
6 **In-A-Gadda-Da-Vida** (17:05)

Total album length: 36 minutes

Iron Butterfly

STEREO

Iron Butterfly

In-A-Gadda-Da-Vida

ATCO
SD 33-250

Blood, Sweat & Tears

| • **Album sales:** 3,000,000 | • **Release date:** August 1969 |

'They ousted me from the band I had envisioned, regrouped with a singer of their choice, and made millions of dollars.' That's how Blood, Sweat & Tears founder Al Kooper recounted the genesis of this Number One album in his autobiography 'Backstage Passes'.

Blood, Sweat & Tears, recorded under the aegis of producer James William Guercio, was the reconstituted band's second long-player. The original group's more adventurous debut album, *Child Is Father To The Man*, was among the first rock-with-horns experiments, but had lacked the commercial punch of *Blood, Sweat & Tears*.

Three top five singles came from the album, 'You've Made Me So Very Happy', was the first gold single, peaking at Number Two. The next single, 'More and More/Spinning Wheel' also peaked at Number Two and went gold. Finally, released in September of 1969, the third gold single from the album, 'And When I Die' also made Number Two by November. It was the first time since the RIAA started certifying gold records that an album had spawned three gold singles. The album reached Number One on the US Charts, staying there for seven weeks, it went double platinum by the end of 1969, and stayed on the Top 40 for 66 weeks.

Number One singles:
None

Grammy awards:
Album of the Year;
Best contemporary
instrumental performance

Label: US: Columbia;
UK: CBS

Recorded in: N/A

Personnel:
David Clayton-Thomas
Steve Katz
Chuck Winfield
Jerry Hyman
Fred Lipsius
Dick Halligan
Jim Fielder
Bobby Colomby
Lew Soloff

Producer:
James William Guercio

1 Variations On A Theme By Eric Satie
   (1st & 2nd Movements) (2:35)
2 Smiling Phases (5:11)
3 Sometimes In Winter (3:09)
4 More And More (3:04)
5 And When I Die (4:06)
6 God Bless The Child (5:55)
7 Spinning Wheel (4:08)
8 You've Made Me So Very Happy (4:19)
0 Blues (Part 2) (11:44)
10 Variations On A Theme By Eric Satie (reprise) (1:49)

Total album length: 42 minutes

Blood, Sweat & Tears

63504

BLOOD, SWEAT & TEARS

12 Crosby, Stills & Nash

| • **Album sales:** 4,000,000 | • **Release date:** June 1969 |

Crosby, Stills & Nash, known by the initials CSN, were one of the most anticipated rock-music debuts of the late 1960s. The public defections of the band's members (David Crosby, Stephen Stills and Graham Nash) from established bands (The Byrds, Buffalo Springfield and Hollies) were a first, introducing the notion of rock musicians as free agents and creating a brief vogue in 'supergroups'. They were one of the few American bands that even came close to rivalling the Beatles in the late 1960s.

Although Nash's incessantly tuneful travelogue 'Marrakesh Express' and Stills' paean to Judy Collins, 'Suite: Judy Blue Eyes', were Top 30 hits, the hippie harmonists initially found their home in the counterculture: FM-rock radio and the festival circuit (the group performed at the Woodstock festival). There is no doubt that Crosby, Stills & Nash's quiet, heavily acoustic songs provided a welcome tonic for audiences overdosed on hard rock and the incessant political turmoil of the period. In 1969, the album sold two million copies, and the group won a Grammy for the year's best new artist.

The trio added Neil Young, Stills' Buffalo Springfield bandmate, to its lineup for 1970's *Deja Vu*. Solo careers have occupied all four principals since the early 1970s, but they have re-formed, in various configurations, for occasional touring and recording.

Number One singles:
None

Grammy Awards: Best new artist of the year

Label: US & UK: Atlantic

Recorded in: N/A

Personnel:
David Crosby
Stephen Stills
Graham Nash
Dallas Taylor

Producer:
Bill Halverson

1 **Suite: Judy Blue Eyes** (7:25)
2 **Marrakesh Express** (2:39)
3 **Guinnevere** (4:40)
4 **You Don't Have To Cry** (2:45)
5 **Pre-Road Downs** (3:01)
6 **Wooden Ships** (5:29)
7 **Lady Of The Island** (2:39)
8 **Helplessly Hoping** (2:41)
9 **Long Time Gone** (4:17)
10 **49 Bye-Byes** (5:16)

Total album length: 40 minutes

Crosby, Stills & Nash

CROSBY, STILLS & NASH

ATLANTIC

STEREO

Meet The Beatles!

| • **Album sales:** 5,000,000 | • **Release date:** January 1964 |

The 1960s' most significant debut still retains much of its initial appeal, both in terms of the sheer originality of its songs and The Beatles invigorating performances. *Meet The Beatles!*, unlike the UK album *With The Beatles* from which it was adapted, is comprised solely of Beatles compositions (excepting 'Till There Was You').

Their first major-label US album, it became America's best-selling LP of all time within a week of its release. In April, The Beatles occupied the top five positions on the US singles chart. *Meet The Beatles!* gave the band their first gold album and their first gold single, 'I Want To Hold Your Hand', on the same day. Obvious highlights are the two sides of the

Lennon–McCartney single that introduced America to the group, the clap-happy 'I Want to Hold Your Hand' and the pulsing 'I Saw Her Standing There'. There's little decline in quality thereafter, as track after sterling track establishes The Beatles' talent and charms.

Meet The Beatles reveals the group's genius at absorbing and synthesizing varying styles into music that is uniquely its own. Thus, the poppy 'All My Loving' uses country elements while the girl-group sounds of the Shirelles inform 'All I've Got To Do'. The album features the first George Harrison composition 'Don't Bother Me'.

Number One singles:
US & UK: I Want To Hold Your Hand

Grammy awards: None

Label: US: Capitol;
UK: Parlophone

Recorded in: London, UK

Personnel:
John Lennon (d. 1980)
Paul McCartney
George Harrison (d. 2001)
Ringo Starr
George Martin

Producer:
George Martin

1 I Want To Hold Your Hand (2:24)
2 I Saw Her Standing There (2:50)
3 This Boy (2:11)
4 It Won't Be Long (2:11)
5 All I've Got To Do (2:05)
6 All My Loving (2:04)
7 Don't Bother Me (2:28)
8 Little Child (1:46)
9 Till There Was You (2:12)
10 Hold Me Tight (2:30)
11 I Wanna Be Your Man (1:59)
12 Not A Second Time (2:03)

Total album length: 27 minutes

The Beatles

MEET THE BEATLES!

The First Album by England's Phenomenal Pop Combo

Capitol
RECORDS

HIGH FIDELITY

Sleeve artwork by Robert Freeman

Revolver

| • **Album sales:** 5,000,000 | • **Release date:** August 1966 |

Regarded widely as one of the greatest pop albums of all time, *Revolver* represents The Beatles' coming of age as songwriters and musicians. Yet another step in the band's continuing effort to go beyond the confines of standard pop-song fodder, *Revolver* is loaded with an eclectic array of subject matter, including Harrison's caustic indictment of an unfair tax system ('Taxman'), McCartney's haunting portrait of a lonely spinster ('Eleanor Rigby') and Lennon's tape-looped rumination 'Tomorrow Never Knows'. Meanwhile 'Here, There And Everywhere' remains one of the band's most affecting love songs. The Beatles also began to explore fully the possibilities of the recording studio on *Revolver*, bringing the material to sonic life with innovative electronic wizardry.

Revolver shot to the top of the charts and stayed there for six weeks, spurred by the double-sided hit single that paired 'Yellow Submarine' (Number Two) with 'Eleanor Rigby' (Number 11). The album also garnered two Grammy Awards: McCartney won for Best Contemporary (R&R) Solo Vocal Performance (for 'Eleanor Rigby'), and Klaus Voormann won for Best Album Cover, Graphic Arts.

Number One singles:
None

Grammy awards:
Paul McCartney, Best contemporary (R&R) solo vocal performance – 'Eleanor Rigby'; Klaus Voormann, Best album cover, graphic arts

Label: US: Capitol; UK: Parlophone

Recorded in: London, UK

Personnel:
John Lennon (d. 1980)
Paul McCartney
George Harrison (d. 2001)
Ringo Starr
George Martin
Anvil Bhagwat

Producer:
George Martin

1 Taxman (2:39)
2 Eleanor Rigby (2:07)
3 I'm Only Sleeping (3:01)
4 Love You To (3:01)
5 Here, There And Everywhere (2:25)
6 Yellow Submarine (2:40)
7 She Said She Said (2:37)
8 Good Day Sunshine (2:09)
9 And Your Bird Can Sing (2:01)
10 For No One (2:01)
11 Doctor Robert (2:15)
12 I Want To Tell You (2:29)
13 Got To Get You Into My Life (2:30)
14 Tomorrow Never Knows (2:57)

Total album length: 35 minutes

REVOLVER

The Monkees

| **Album sales:** 5,000,000 | **Release date:** January 1967 |

The Monkees' debut was the first of four consecutive US Number Ones for the group, and also topped the UK charts. Assembled by television producers Bob Rafelson and Bert Schneider to portray a Beatles-type pop band on a new series, the quartet recorded (vocals only) between rehearsals for the weekly show.

While subsequent albums would improve on its quality, largely due to the group's increased participation, *The Monkees* remains an appealing mix of pop songs and performances. Mickey Dolenz delivers a rousing lead on the brisk 'Last Train To Clarksville', a US Number One single and one of several tunes written by veteran hitmakers Tommy Boyce and Bobby Hart, while Davy Jones handles the ballad 'I Wanna Be Free'. Mike Nesmith, the member with the most extensive musical background, sings lead on his own country-flavoured compositions, 'Papa Gene's Blues' and 'Sweet Young Thing' (co-written with the legendary Gerry Goffin/Carole King team).

Though critics disparaged the Monkees as the 'Pre-Fab Four', the TV series was a hit. The symbiotic relationship between the show and the records' radio play enabled The Monkees to hold down the top-selling album slot for 13 weeks.

Number One singles:
US: Last Train To Clarksville (UK: unreleased)

Grammy awards:
None

Label: US: Colgems; UK: RCA Victor

Recorded in: Hollywood, USA

Personnel:
Davy Jones
Mickey Dolenz
Mike Nesmith
Peter Tork
Various other musicians

Producers:
Tommy Boyce
Bobby Hart
Jack Keller
Mike Nesmith

1 (Theme From) The Monkees (2:21)
2 Saturday's Child (2:45)
3 I Wanna Be Free (2:27)
4 Tomorrow's Gonna Be Another Day (2:39)
5 Papa Gene's Blues (2:00)
6 Take A Giant Step (2:31)
7 Last Train To Clarksville (2:47)
8 This Just Doesn't Seem To Be My Day (2:09)
9 Let's Dance On (2:32)
10 I'll Be True To You (2:49)
11 Sweet Young Thing (1:58)
12 Gonna Buy Me A Dog (2:44)

Album length: 30 minutes

mono RD-7844

RCA VICTOR | RCA

the MONKEES

(theme from) THE MONKEES/Saturday's Child
I Wanna Be Free/Tomorrow's Gonna Be Another Day
Papa Gene's Blues/Take a Giant Step
Last Train to Clarksville/This Just Doesn't Seem to Be My Day
Let's Dance On/I'll Be True to You
Sweet Young Thing/Gonna Buy Me a Dog

8 More Of The Monkees

| • **Album sales:** 5,000,000 | • **Release date:** April 1967 |

Like their debut, the second set by The Monkees was a top-ranking album in the US (for 18 weeks); it also went to Number One on the UK charts. Though the group's role remains limited to singing, *More Of The Monkees* is a measurably better record, thanks in part to Neil Diamond whose composition 'I'm A Believer' was the group's second Number One single. Another Diamond song, and one of the album's obvious high points is 'Look Out (Here Comes Tomorrow)'. The track rests squarely in the rock 'n' roll camp, as does Boyce and Hart's 1960s garage-rock classic '(I'm Not Your) Steppin' Stone'. The tune get a ferocious treatment from Dolenz, who reveals himself to be one of the period's most underrated vocalists.

Within weeks of the album's release, Nesmith lobbied, successfully, with *The Monkees* TV-show producer Bob Rafelson for the group to be allowed to play, as well as sing, on forthcoming records. The TV series *The Monkees* won the Emmy for Best Comedy 1966.

Number One singles:
US & UK: I'm A Believer

Grammy Awards: None

Label: US: Colgems;
UK: RCA Victor

Recorded in:
Los Angeles, USA

Personnel:
Mike Nesmith
Micky Dolenz
Peter Tork
Davy Jones
Artie Butler

Bill Lewis
Don Randi
Gary Coleman
Hal Blaine
Neil Sedaka
Norm Jeffries
Various other personnel

Producers:
Tommy Boyce
Neil Sedaka
Michael Nesmith
Jack Keller
Gerry Goffin
Carole Bayer Sager
Carole King
Bobby Hart

1   **When Love Comes Knockin' (At Your Door) (1:49)**
2   **Mary, Mary (2:16)**
3   **Hold On Girl (2:29)**
4   **Your Auntie Grizelda (2:30)**
5   **(I'm Not Your) Steppin' Stone (2:25)**
6   **Look Out (Here Comes Tomorrow) (2:16)**
7   **The Kind Of Girl I Could Love (1:53)**
8   **The Day We Fell In Love (2:26)**
9   **Sometime In The Morning (2:30)**
10 **Laugh (2:30)**
11 **I'm A Believer (2:50)**

Total album length: 26 minutes

The Monkees

Rubber Soul

| • **Album sales:** 6,000,000 | • **Release date:** December 1965 |

Two years of unbridled Beatlemania had afforded the Fab Four considerable career clout. On *Rubber Soul*, the group's 1965 yuletide offering, they began to display that confidence, stretching out musically – not even bothering to put their name on the album's cover.

Gone were the echo-drenched, electrified big-beat performances and teen love anthems of previous years, replaced with a more mature, acoustic-guitar-driven sound and introspective lyrical slant. Highlights include Lennon's 'Norwegian Wood (This Bird Has Flown)', a thinly veiled reference to an extra-marital affair, with sitar by George Harrison; 'In My Life', a poignant memory-lane trip; and 'I'm Looking Through You', McCartney's swipe at then-current

girlfriend, British actress Jane Asher. Paul's faux-French ballad 'Michelle' garnered Lennon and McCartney a Grammy for Song of the Year.

Topping the charts for six weeks, the US version of *Rubber Soul* opens on a different note than its UK counterpart, starting with the more acoustic, country-styled 'I've Just Seen A Face' (a leftover from the British edition of the *Help!* album). The UK version of the album begins with the Anglo-soul strut 'Drive My Car'.

Number One singles:
None

Grammy Awards: Song of the year – Michelle

Label: US: Capitol;
UK: Parlophone

Recorded in: London, UK

Personnel:
John Lennon (d. 1980)
Paul McCartney
George Harrison (d. 2001)
Ringo Starr
George Martin
Mal Evans

Producer:
George Martin

US:
1 I've Just Seen A Face (2:04)
2 Norwegian Wood (This Bird Has Flown) (2:00)
3 You Won't See Me (3:19)
4 Think For Yourself (2:16)
5 The Word (2:43)
6 Michelle (2:42)
7 It's Only Love (1:53)
8 Girl (2:26)
9 I'm Looking Through You (2:27)
10 In My Life (2:27)
11 Wait (2:16)
12 Run For Your Life (2:18)

Total album length: 29 minutes

UK:
1 Drive My Car (2:30)
2 Norwegian Wood (This Bird Has Flown) (2:00)
3 You Won't See Me (3:19)
4 Nowhere Man (2:44)
5 Think For Yourself (2:16)
6 The Word (2:42)
7 Michelle (2:42)
8 What Goes On? (2:50)
9 Girl (2:33)
10 I'm Looking Through You (2:27)
11 In My Life (2:27)
12 Wait (2:16)
13 If I Need Someone (2:23)
14 Run For Your Life (2:18)

Total album length: 35 minutes

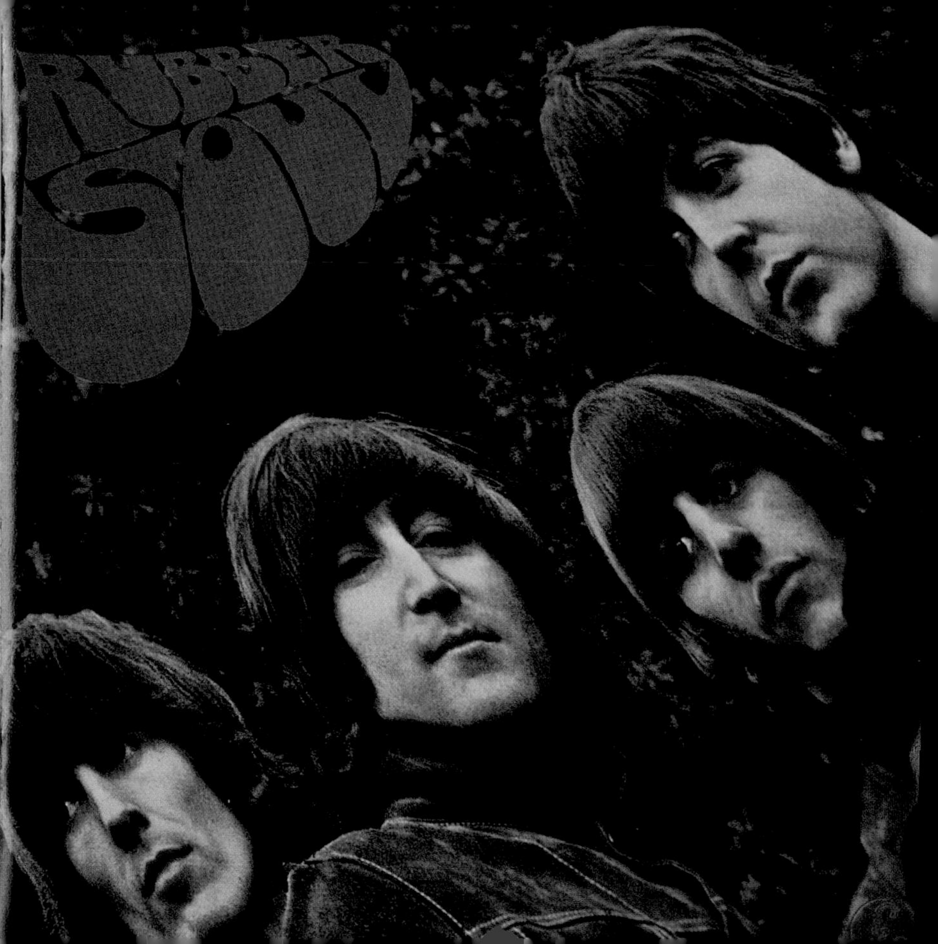

Sleeve artwork by Robert Freeman

Magical Mystery Tour

| • **Album sales:** 6,000,000 | • **Release date:** December 1967 |

In 1967, another chart-topping Beatles album seemed par for the course. The soundtrack to the group's British television special (the first to air worldwide) was, sequentially, the follow-up to *Sgt. Pepper*, issued that summer. While *Magical Mystery Tour* might suffer in cut-by-cut comparison to this acknowledged masterpiece, it's nonetheless a compelling set, due mainly to the presence of all six sides of the Beatles' most recent – and highly adventurous – singles. These include the sublime 'Penny Lane' (Number One in the US and Number Two in the UK), 'All You Need Is Love' (Number One on both sides of the Atlantic) and 'Hello Goodbye'.

In addition to these tracks and the album's psychedelic title cut, the program features 'The Fool On The Hill', notable for one of McCartney's most moving vocals, the wordless 'Flying' and Harrison's eerie, fog-bound 'Blue Jay Way'. McCartney's 'Your Mother Should Know' harks back to such music-hall salutes as *Sgt. Pepper*'s 'When I'm Sixty-Four'.

In the UK, *Magical Mystery Tour* was issued as a double ep [extended-play single]. While the soundtrack, in both its US and UK forms, was an artistic and commercial success, the Beatles' TV special took a beating from critics, who found it plotless and confusing.

Number One singles:
US & UK: All You Need Is Love; Hello Goodbye;
US: Penny Lane

Grammy Awards:
None

Label: US: Capitol;
UK: Parlophone

Recorded in: London, UK

Personnel:
John Lennon (d. 1980)
Paul McCartney
George Harrison (d. 2001)
Ringo Starr

Producer:
George Martin

1 **Magical Mystery Tour** (2:51)
2 **Fool On The Hill** (3:00)
3 **Flying** (2:16)
4 **Blue Jay Way** (3:56)
5 **Your Mother Should Know** (2:29)
6 **I Am The Walrus** (4:37)
7 **Hello Goodbye** (3:31)
8 **Strawberry Fields Forever** (4:10)
9 **Penny Lane** (3:03)
10 **Baby You're A Rich Man** (3:03)
11 **All You Need Is Love** (3:48)

Total album length: 37 minutes

Magical Mystery Tour
The Fool On The Hill Flying Blue Jay Way
Your Mother Should Know I Am The Walrus
MAGICAL MYSTERY TOUR
Includes 24-page full color picture book
Hello Goodbye Strawberry Fields Forever
Penny Lane Baby You're A Rich Man
All You Need Is Love

Led Zeppelin

| • **Album sales:** 10,000,000 | • **Release date:** January 1969 |

*L*ed Zeppelin remains one of the most auspicious and influential debuts in pop. Countless late-1960s rock bands had toiled in the blues field, particularly as psychedelic rock mutated into 'heavy rock', but none with so original and outsized a take on the venerable genre as Led Zeppelin. The album was recorded in 30 hours, it cost a mere £1,782 ($3,198) and by 1975 would gross £3,500,000 ($6,300,000).

Structurally, all the music on *Led Zeppelin* is blues, but the band's treatment of the form is expansive. Tempos are slowed to allow the riffs to gather force and explode with gales of guitar and shrieking vocals, as on the classics 'You Shook Me' and 'Dazed And Confused'.

Acoustic elements are allowed into the traditional folk song 'Babe I'm Gonna Leave You', and 'Black Mountain Side' is a quiet, all-instrumental interlude, but the album is mostly thunderous and unrelenting in its energy and attack. As such the album – and its sequel, *Led Zeppelin II* – has been a source of inspiration to generations of young musicians eager to express such power before audiences.

Led Zeppelin reached Number Six in the album charts in the UK and spent 79 weeks on chart. It reached Number 10 in the US spending 50 weeks on chart.

Number One singles:
None

Grammy awards:
None

Label:
US & UK: Atlantic

Recorded in: London, UK

Personnel:
Jimmy Page
Robert Plant
John Paul Jones
Jon Bonham (d. 1980)
Sandy Denny
Viram Jasani

Producers:
Jimmy Page
Peter Grant (d. 1995)

1 Good Times Bad Times (2:43)
2 Babe I'm Gonna Leave You (6:40)
3 You Shook Me (6:30)
4 Dazed And Confused (6:27)
5 Your Time Is Gonna Come (4:41)
6 Black Mountain Side (2:06)
7 Communication Breakdown (2:26)
8 I Can't Quit You Baby (4:42)
9 How Many More Times (3:30)

Total album length: 40 minutes

Led Zeppelin

LED ZEPPELIN

Sleeve artwork by George Hardie

ATLANTIC

Sgt. Pepper's Lonely Hearts Club Band

| • **Album sales:** 11,000,000 | • **Release date:** June 1967 |

When The Beatles first arrived in America in February 1964, the magazine *Newsweek* labelled their lyrics 'a catastrophe' and their music 'a near disaster'. Three years later, the same publication was comparing them to T.S. Eliot, Wordsworth, and Tennyson. *Sgt. Pepper* was the occasion for the change of heart.

Both *Rubber Soul* (1965) and *Revolver* (1966) had revealed a steep increase in the sophistication of The Beatles' songwriting and recording skills, but neither was as ambitious – or successful at realizing its ambitions – as *Sgt. Pepper*. The album, which was recorded at London's Abbey Road studios using a pioneering eight-track recording process, made Number One in both the UK and US albums charts. Embracing styles as far apart as music-hall ('With A Little Help from My Friends'), psychedelia ('A Day In The Life,' 'Lucy In The Sky With Diamonds'), Indian ('Within You, Without You') and turn-of-the-century nostalgia ('When I'm Sixty-Four'), *Sgt. Pepper* held the top position for 15 weeks and remained on the charts for nearly three-and-a-half years.

The album sleeve, which was the first to feature a gatefold design and complete song lyrics, is also notable for Peter Blake's distinctive artwork, featuring wax models of the Beatles from London's Madame Tussauds.

Number One singles:
None

Grammys awards:
Album of the year; Best contemporary album

Label: US: Capitol;
UK: Parlophone

Recorded in: London, UK

Personnel:
John Lennon (d. 1980)
Paul McCartney
George Harrison (d. 2001)
Ringo Starr
Geoff Emerick

Producer:
George Martin

1 Sgt. Pepper's Lonely Hearts Club Band (2.02)
2 With A Little Help From My Friends (2.44)
3 Lucy In The Sky With Diamonds (3.29)
4 Getting Better (2.48)
5 Fixing A Hole (2.36)
6 She's Leaving Home (3.35)
7 Being For The Benefit Of Mr. Kite (2.37)
8 Within You, Without You (5.06)
9 When I'm Sixty-Four (2.37)
10 Lovely Rita (2.42)
11 Good Morning, Good Morning (2.42)
12 Sgt. Pepper's Lonely Heart's Club Band (Reprise) (1.19)
13 A Day In The Life (5.33)

Total album length: 40 minutes

The Beatles

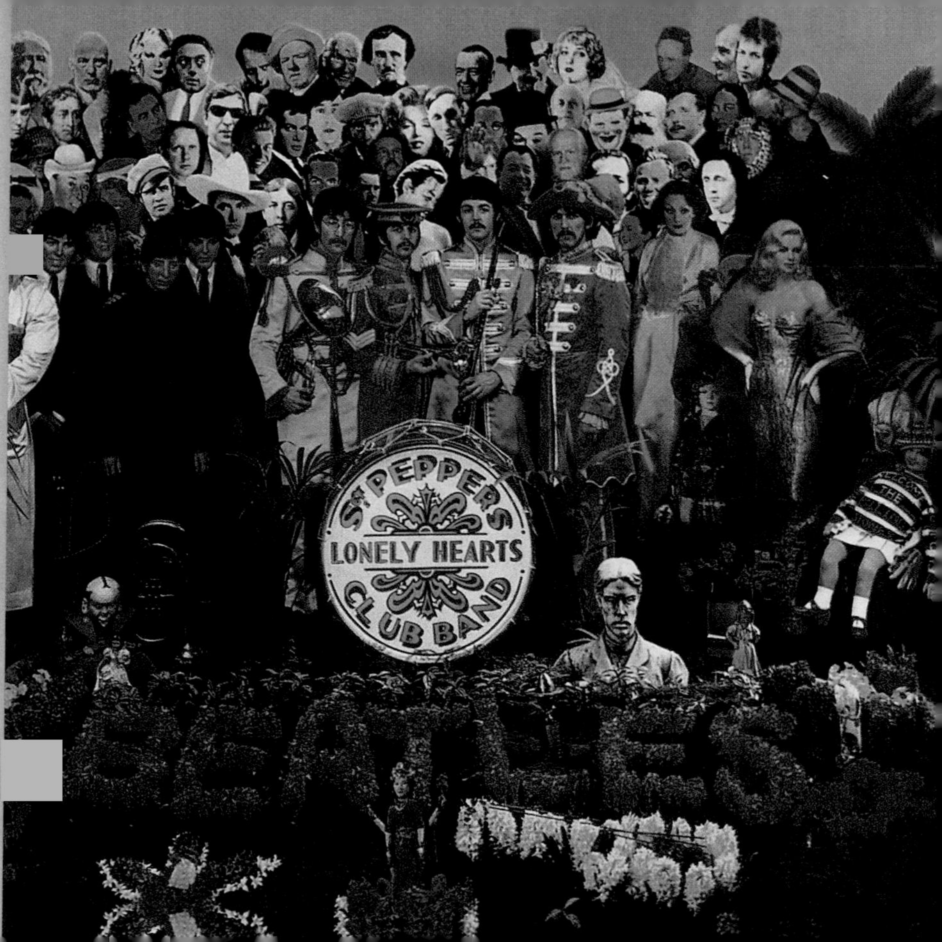

Sleeve artwork by Peter Blake and Michael Cooper

Abbey Road

| • **Album sales:** 12,000,000 | • **Release date:** October 1969 |

Though *Let It Be* was The Beatles' last official album release, *Abbey Road* was their real swan song, a fitting cap to their career and the decade they dominated. Lennon announced to the other Beatles that he was leaving the band soon after *Let It Be* but was persuaded to remain quiet in public. Shaking off the creative malaise that had stalled them the group temporarily shelved that project and reconvened at Abbey Road studios with renewed musical vigour.

The album is divided into two distinct halves, with the first side comprising stand-alone tracks (opening with Lennon's 'Come Together') and the second featuring an adventurous song suite that justifies its musical pretensions. George Harrison also steps out of Lennon and McCartney's

shadow on this LP, penning the album's two best songs, the ebullient 'Here Comes The Sun' and the ballad 'Something'.

A Grammy winner – for Best Engineered Recording – this 1969 release logged 11 straight weeks at Number One. However the single 'Something' failed to top of the charts, reaching Number Three in the US and Four in the UK.

Number One singles:
None

Grammy awards: Best engineered (non-classical) recording

Label: US & UK: Apple

Recorded in: London, UK

Personnel:
John Lennon (d. 1980)
Paul McCartney
George Harrison (d. 2001)
Ringo Starr

Producer:
George Martin

1 Come Together (4:20)
2 Maxwell's Silver Hammer (3:27)
3 Something (3:03)
4 Oh Darling (3:26)
5 Octopus's Garden (2:51)
6 I Want You (She's So Heavy) (7:47)
7 Here Comes The Sun (3:05)
8 Because (2:45)
9 You Never Give Me Your Money (4:02)
10 Sun King (2:26)
11 Mean Mr Mustard (1:06)
12 Polythene Pam (1:12)
13 She Came In Through The Bathroom Window (1:57)
14 Golden Slumbers (1:31)
15 Carry That Weight (1:36)
16 The End (2:19)
17 Her Majesty (0:23)

Total album length: 47 minutes

The Beatles

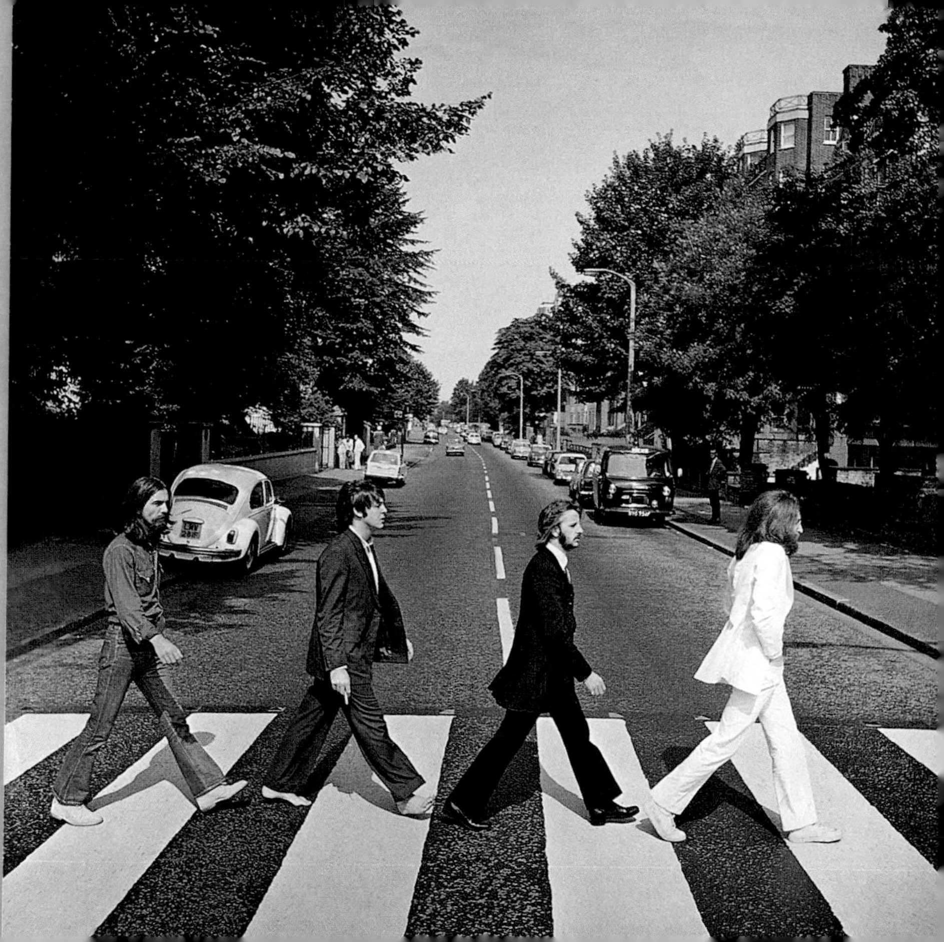

Sleeve artwork by Ian MacMillan

Led Zeppelin II

| • **Album sales:** 12,000,000 | • **Release date:** October 1969 |

In January 1969 Led Zeppelin got the ball running with the release of their debut album in January. Only nine months later they released their second album, *Led Zeppelin II*. It proved even more popular than the first, eventually selling 12,000,000 copies and hitting Number One in both the US and UK, where it enjoyed chart runs of 98 and 138 weeks, respectively.

Led Zeppelin II was recorded during the band's US tour and probably owes much of its success to their popularity as a live act. A hit single was also a factor. Though *Led Zeppelin* and *Led Zeppelin II* both received widespread airplay on album-oriented FM stations, the release of 'Whole Lotta Love' as a single took the band's powerful sound to the larger Top 40 AM-radio audience as well. 'Whole Lotta Love' reached Number Four in the US.

The album does not deviate greatly from the approach introduced on the band's debut set. 'Ramble On' is largely acoustic and bare-boned in its arrangement, but the bulk of the program relies on muscle and electricity. *Rolling Stone* magazine voted the album Number 75 in the 500 greatest albums of all time.

Number One singles:
None

Grammy awards: None

Label: US & UK: Atlantic

Recorded in: Various locations, USA

Producer:
Peter Grant (d. 1995)

Personnel:
Jimmy Page
John Bonham (d. 1980)
John Paul Jones
Robert Plant
Andy Johns
Chris Huston
Eddie Kramer
George Chkiantz
George Marino

1. Whole Lotta Love (5:34)
2. What Is And What Should Never Be (4:44)
3. Lemon Song (6:19)
4. Thank You (4:47)
5. Heartbreaker (4:14)
6. Living Loving Maid (She's Just a Woman) (2:39)
7. Ramble On (4:23)
8. Moby Dick (4:21)
9. Bring It On Home (4:20)

Total album length: 41 minutes

Led Zeppelin

STEREO

Led Zeppelin II

40 037
(SD 8236)

ATLANTIC

Sleeve artwork by David Juniper

The Beatles (The 'White' Album)

| • Album sales: 19,000,000 | • Release date: November 1968 |

In May of 1968, The Beatles gathered at George Harrison's house to record demos and take stock of the wealth of material they had amassed from their recent stay in India. Most of the songs from this time would end up on the mammoth double-album *The Beatles*, commonly known as the 'white' album, released that November.

The album's stark monochromatic cover (with the blind-embossed title intentionally set at an angle) is visually arresting, but it also provides some indication of the disharmony within the foursome who could not agree on a visual image. Something of this tension can be heard on the album, which is noticeably less cohesive than earlier efforts; producer George Martin has said it would've made a better single disc. By this time, the songwriters were beginning to head in their own directions; John Lennon with the soulful 'Julia', Paul McCartney with 'Back in the USSR', and George Harrison with the beautiful 'While My Guitar Gently Weeps', featuring Eric Clapton.

The album reached Number One on both sides of the Atlantic.

Number One singles:
None

Grammy Awards: None

Label:
US & UK: Apple

Recorded in:
London, UK

Producer:
George Martin

Personnel:
John Lennon (d. 1980)
Paul McCartney
George Harrison (d. 2001)
Ringo Starr
Yoko Ono
Eric Clapton
Mal Evans
George Martin
Chris Thomas
Maureen Starkey
Patti Harrison

1 Back In The USSR (2:43)
2 Dear Prudence (3:57)
3 Glass Onion (2:17)
4 Ob-la-di-ob-la-da (3:09)
5 Wild Honey Pie (1:02)
6 The Continuing Story Of Bungalo Bill (3:05)
7 While My Guitar Gently Weeps (4:45)
8 Happiness Is A Warm Gun (2:44)
9 Martha My Dear (2:29)
10 I'm So Tired (2:03)
11 Blackbird (2:18)
12 Piggies (2:05)
13 Rocky Racoon (3:41)
14 Don't Pass Me By (3:42)
15 Why Don't We Do It In The Road? (1:41)
16 I Will (1:47)
17 Julia (2:54)
18 Birthday (2:43)
19 Yer Blues (4:01)
20 Mother Nature's Son (2:48)
21 Everybody's Got Something To Hide Except Me And My Monkey (2:25)
22 Sexy Sadie (3:15)
23 Helter Skelter (4:30)
24 Long Long Long (3:04)
25 Revolution 1 (4:16)
26 Honey Pie (2:41)
27 Savoy Truffle (2:55)
28 Cry Baby Cry (3:11)
29 Revolution 9 (8:13)
30 Good Night (3:12)

Total album length: 94 minutes

The BEATLES

Appendix: Facts and figures

The 20 highest-ranking US artists (position on list given in brackets)

1 The Monkees: *More Of The Monkees* (8)
2 Crosby, Stills & Nash: *Crosby, Stills & Nash* (12)
3 Blood, Sweat & Tears: *Blood, Sweat & Tears* (13)
4 Iron Butterfly: *In-A-Gadda-Da-Vida* (14)
5 Jimi Hendrix: *Are You Experienced?* (15)
6 Creedence Clearwater Revival: *Green River* (18)
7 Johnny Cash: *At San Quentin* (19)
8 Simon & Garfunkel: *Parsley, Sage, Rosemary & Thyme* (21)
9 Elvis Presley: *Blue Hawaii* (26)
10 Chicago: *Chicago Transit Authority* (29)
11 Santana: *Santana* (30)
12 Glen Campbell: *Witchita Lineman* (33)
13 Big Brother & The Holding Company: *Cheap Thrills* (35)
14 The Doors: *The Doors* (40)
15 Bob Dylan: *Blonde On Blonde* (41)
16 Peter, Paul & Mary: *Peter, Paul & Mary* (45)
17 Sly & The Family Stone: *Stand!* (49)
18 Barbra Streisand: *Funny Girl* (58)
19 Frank Sinatra: *Strangers In The Night* (68)
20 The Beach Boys: *Pet Sounds* (69)

The 10 highest-ranking UK or international artists

1 The Beatles: *The Beatles* [White Album] (1)
2 Led Zeppelin: *Led Zeppelin II* (2)
3 Van Morrison: *Moondance* (17)
4 The Rolling Stones: *Let It Bleed* (27)
5 The Who: *Tommy* (32)
6 The Band: *The Band* (46)
7 Blind Faith: *Blind Faith* (48)
8 The Moody Blues: *On The Threshold Of A Dream* (51)
9 Cream: *Disraeli Gears* (65)
10 The Singing Nun: *The Singing Nun* (95)

Live albums in the Top 100

1 *At San Quentin*: Johnny Cash (19)
2 *At Folsom Prison*: Johnny Cash (20)
3 *Wonderfulness*: Bill Cosby (70)
4 *Bill Cosby Is A Very Funny Fellow, Right!*: Bill Cosby (78)

The 10 highest-ranking solo artists

1 Van Morrison: *Moondance* (17)
2 Johnny Cash: *Johnny Cash At San Quentin* (19)
3 Elvis Presley: *Blue Hawaii* (26)
4 Glen Campbell: *Wichita Lineman* (33)
5 Bob Dylan: *Blonde on Blonde* (41)
6 Frank Sinatra: *Strangers In The Night* (68)
7 Bill Crosby: *Wonderfulness* (70)
8 Barbra Streisand: *My Name Is Barbra* (72)
9 Ray Coniff: *We Wish You A Merry Christmas* (79)
10 Nat King Cole: *Ramblin' Rose* (80)

The 10 highest-ranking bands

1 The Beatles: *The Beatles* [White Album] (1)
2 Led Zeppelin: *Led Zeppelin II* (2)
3 The Monkees: *More Of The Monkees* (8)
4 Crosby, Stills & Nash: *Crosby, Stills & Nash* (12)
5 Blood, Sweat & Tears: *Blood, Sweat & Tears* (13)
6 Iron Butterfly: *In-A-Gadda-Da-Vida* (14)
7 The Jimi Hendrix Experience: *Are You Experienced?* (15)
8 Creedence Clearwater Revival: *Green River* (18)
9 Simon & Garfunkel: *Parsley, Sage, Rosemary & Thyme* (21)
10 The Rolling Stones: *Let It Bleed* (27)

Record labels with the most albums in the Top 100

1 Capitol (21 albums)
2 CBS (20 albums)
3 Columbia (19 albums)
4 Parlophone (10 albums)
5 RCA (9 albums)
6 RCA/Victor (8 albums)
7 Warners (6 albums)
8 Colgems (5 albums)
9 Decca (5 albums)
10 Atlantic (4 albums)
11 Elektra (4 albums)
12 London (4 albums)
13 Reprise (4 albums)
14 Apple (3 albums)
15 Atco (3 albums)
16 EMI (3 albums)
17 Fantasy (3 albums)
18 Liberty (3 albums)
19 Polydor (3 albums)
20 Track (3 albums)

Artists with the most albums in the Top 100
(artists ranked by number of albums and aggregate score of album positions)

1   The Beatles
The Beatles [White Album] (1)
Abbey Road (3)
Sgt. Pepper's Lonely Heart Club Band (4)
Magical Mystery Tour (6)
Rubber Soul (7)
Revolver (10)
Meet The Beatles (11)
Hard Day's Night (16)
Beatles '65 (23)
Help! (24)
Yesterday & Today (42)
Second Album (44)
Yellow Submarine (53)

2   Bob Dylan
Blonde On Blonde (41)
Nashville Skyline (50)
John Wesley Harding (60)
Highway 61 Revisited (74)
Bringing It All Back Home (75)
The Freewheelin' Bob Dylan (76)

3   The Monkees
More Of The Monkees (8)
The Monkees (9)
Pisces, Aquarius, Capricorn & Jones Ltd (37)
Headquarters (38)
The Birds, The Bees & The Monkees (59)

4   Elvis Presley
Blue Hawaii (26)
How Great Art Thou (39)
His Hand In Mine (81)
GI Blues (82)
Roustabout (92)

5   Simon & Garfunkel
Parsley, Sage, Rosemary & Thyme (21)
Sounds Of Silence (22)
The Graduate (34)
Bookends (36)

6   The Doors
The Doors (40)
Soft Parade (47)
Waiting For The Sun (57)
Strange Days (62)

7   Glen Campbell
Wichita Lineman (33)
Galveston (52)
By The Time I Get To Phoenix (63)
Gentle On My Mind (67)

8   The Rolling Stones
Let It Bleed (27)
Beggar's Banquet (54)
Aftermath (71)
Out Of Our Heads (73)

Soundtrack albums in the Top 100

1 *Magical Mystery Tour*: The Beatles (6)
2 *A Hard Day's Night*: The Beatles (16)
3 *Help!*: The Beatles (24)
4 *West Side Story*: Various Artists (25)
5 *Blue Hawaii*: Elvis Presley (26)
6 *The Graduate*: Simon & Garfunkel (34)
7 *Fiddler On The Roof*: Various Artists (43)
8 *Yellow Submarine*: The Beatles (53)
9 *Romeo & Juliet*: Nino Rota (56)
10 *Funny Girl*: Barbra Streisand (58)
11 *Camelot*: Various Artists(66)
12 *GI Blues*: Elvis Presley (82)
13 *Hair*: Various Artists (85)
14 *Dr Zhivago*: Maurice Jarre (90)
15 *The Sound Of Music*: Various Artists (91)
16 *Goldfinger*: Various Artists (93)
17 *Mary Poppins*: Various Artists (94)
18 *Roustabout*: Elvis Presley (92)
19 *Breakfast At Tiffany's*: Henry Mancini (99)

Albums winning multiple-Grammy awards

1 *Breakfast At Tiffany's*: Henry Mancini (5 Grammys)
2 *At Folsom Prison*: Johnny Cash (3 Grammys)
3 *By The Time I Get To Phoenix*: Glen Campbell
   (3 Grammys)
4 *Ode To Billy Joe*: Bobbie Gentry (3 Grammys)
5 *Sgt. Pepper's Lonely Hearts Club Band*: The Beatles
   (2 Grammys)
6 *Revolver*: The Beatles (2 Grammys)
7 *Blood, Sweat & Tears*: Blood, Sweat & Tears
   (2 Grammys)
8 *The Graduate*: Simon & Garfunkel (2 Grammys)
9 *How Great Art Thou*: Elvis Presley (2 Grammys)
10 *Peter, Paul & Mary*: Peter, Paul & Mary (2 Grammys)
11 *Gentle On My Mind*: Glen Campbell (2 Grammys)
12 *Strangers In The Night*: Frank Sinatra (2 Grammys)
13 *The First Family*: Vaughn Meader (2 Grammys)
14 *The Button-Down Mind Of Bob Newhart*: Bob Newhart
   (2 Grammys)

Index